SIX
Ingredients
or Less

Chicken
Cookbook

SIX
Ingredients
or Less
Chicken
Cookbook

Carlean Johnson

CJ
BOOKS
Washington

Six Ingredients Or Less
Chicken Cookbook

Typography and production design: Linda Hazen
Cover design by Judy Petry
Cover photo by Fred Milkie

ISBN 0-942878-02-7

C. J. Books
P.O. Box 922
Gig Harbor, WA 98335
206-851-3778

To Mom and Dad

ACKNOWLEDGMENTS

The process of putting together a cookbook is quite involved. It is something one person could never do alone. There are many I would like to thank for making this book possible.

My daughter Linda Hazen has been my right arm thoughout the writing of this cookbook. I could not have done it without her. I appreciate the many hours she spent, almost daily, in front of the computer, designing the inside of the book and making sure everything came together. Linda and her husband Joe sampled so many chicken recipes it's a wonder they still like chicken.

I would also like to thank Judy Petry for the cover design. We had lots of fun and laughs shopping for the best looking raw chicken, then deciding how to make it look attractive for the cover. Judy not only did a beautiful book cover, but also came to our rescue when we weren't sure if we could meet our deadline.

I sincerely want to thank Margaret Foster-Finan for the back cover copy and Pattie Graffe and Llewellyn Ernst for the many hours spent in proof-reading.

ABOUT THE AUTHOR

Carlean Johnson, mother of three, resides in scenic Gig Harbor in the Puget Sound area of Washington State. For as long as she can remember, cooking and experimenting with recipes has been her hobby. With our ever changing lifestyles, we do not have time to spend long hours in the kitchen planning meals from lengthy and complicated recipes. Carlean saw a real need for a different type of cookbook; one that would get you in and out of the kitchen fast and yet could be a gourmet's delight or just a simple Sunday supper. Thus was born Six Ingredients Or Less, a best-selling one of a kind cookbook followed by Six Ingredients Or Less Chicken Cookbook.

TABLE OF CONTENTS

Helpful Hints

With todays busy schedules, most of us prefer to plan meals that are quick and easy to prepare. A few minutes of planning will make meal-time a pleasure rather than a crisis.

Preparing a planned menu may take less time and effort than deciding on a restaurant or standing in line for "fast food". Many of us are turning to TV dinners, but a steady diet of those and you may be ready for what I call "real food".

The following hints will help you use this cookbook as well as make meal-time run more smoothly:

1. Always read a recipe through before making out your grocery list or preparing the recipe. You don't want any surprises such as marinating or chilling or discovering at the last minute that you do not have all the ingredients on hand.

2. Most of the recipes make 4 to 6 servings, but can easily be increased or decreased. It is important to note that these are servings, not people. One hungry teenager could possibly eat 2 or 3 servings of some things and smaller appetites could stretch a recipe to make more servings.

3. If necessary, allow time for butter, cream cheese and eggs to come to room temperature. This is important for most cakes and desserts.

4. Pie crusts from scratch are usually preferred, if you have time, but purchased ones are convenient to have on hand.

INTRODUCTION

There are many new and exciting ways to cook chicken. It is one of the tastiest and most versatile choices for family meals, company dinners and holiday entertaining. You can't go wrong with chicken as it is a favorite with almost everyone.

This cookbook was designed for the cook who enjoys cooking with chicken, but doesn't have a lot of time. A minimum of ingredients, simply prepared, does make cooking with chicken fast and almost effortless.

In my original cookbook, Six Ingredients Or Less, some comments were made about the use of canned soup in some of the recipes. Several people told me emphatically that they did not use canned soup. In the revision, I omitted most of the recipes calling for soup and you can probably guess what happened next. Everyone cried, "You left out some of my favorite recipes, I use them all the time!" In this cookbook, I decided to give recipes with soup their own section. If you cook with soup, you will enjoy it, if not, go on to the next section.

The menu section is a result of so many requests for menu ideas and grocery lists. The menus have been selected for your convenience, but feel free to switch recipes around or substitute. Most of the recipes can be increased or decreased, but remember to adjust the grocery list accordingly.

By adding your own personal touches, these recipes can be enjoyed in your kitchen year 'round.

Happy Cooking!

Carlean Johnson
Gig Harbor, Washington

Appetizers

APPETIZER CHICKEN WINGS

OVEN

> **20 chicken wings, cut in half (discard tip)**
> **$1/4$ cup catsup**
> **2 tablespoons honey**
> **2 tablespoons soy sauce**
> **2 tablespoons lemon juice**

Place chicken wings on greased shallow baking sheet. Combine remaining ingredients; brush some of the mixture over the chicken. Bake at 350° for 20 minutes. Turn and baste with sauce. Continue baking 20 minutes, basting occasionally, until chicken is tender and richly glazed.

TIP: Chicken wings can be prepared ahead and marinated in the sauce 2 to 3 hours before baking.

CHICKEN NUGGETS

TOP OF STOVE

These will be popular for a long time.

> **2 whole chicken breast halves, skinned and boned**
> **1 cup flour**
> **1 teaspoon paprika**
> **Salt and pepper**
> **1 egg**
> **Oil**

Cut chicken into $1^{1}/2$-inch pieces. Combine flour, paprika, salt and pepper in small bowl. In another small bowl, mix egg with about 1 tablespoon water. Heat oil, about 2-inches, in deep saucepan or skillet. Oil should be about 350°. Coat chicken pieces in flour mixture, dip in egg, coat again with flour mixture. Carefully drop a few pieces at a time in the oil; cook until tender and lightly browned. This won't take long, 2 to 3 minutes depending on how hot the oil is. Serve with Sweet-Sour Sauce, page 51. Makes about 24 appetizers.

TIP: Overcooking will cause the chicken to be tough, stringy and dry.

TERIYAKI CHICKEN WINGS   OVEN

A nice recipe that can be made ahead and reheated.

> **20 chicken wings, cut in half (discard tips)**
> **1 cup soy sauce**
> **1 cup sugar**
> **2 tablespoons fresh lemon juice**
> **$^1/_8$ teaspoon ground ginger**
> **3 small cloves garlic, minced**

Place chicken wings, skin-side down, on large flat-type baking pan (like a jelly roll pan). Combine remaining ingredients; stir to dissolve sugar. Pour over chicken wings. Bake at 300° for 30 minutes. Turn wings and continue baking 30 minutes. Increase heat to 350° and bake 10 to 15 minutes, basting frequently with the sauce. Makes about 15 to 20 servings.

TIP: If these are made ahead, strain the sauce and save. To reheat, pour sauce over wings in baking pan and bake at 350° until heated through. Or put in a large skillet or wok; toss with some of the sauce and cook until heated through. Leftover sauce can also be used as a dipping sauce for the chicken wings.

GREEN CHILES AND CHEESE DIP   TOP OF STOVE

Serves a lot of people and takes only a few minutes to make.

> **1 cup cubed cooked chicken (small cubes)**
> **1 (8-ounce) package cream cheese, softened**
> **3 (5-ounce) jars Old English cheese (Kraft)**
> **1 cup medium hot salsa**
> **1 (4-ounce) can diced green chiles**

Combine ingredients in medium saucepan. Cook over low heat until cheese is melted, stirring frequently. Serve with the large size corn chips or Doritoes.

TIP: Can make ahead and reheat. Leftovers can be frozen.

VARIATION: Increase chicken to $1^1/_2$ cups, cut into larger cubes. Serve over hot baked potatoes.

ARTICHOKE DIP WITH CHICKEN   TOP OF STOVE

Delicious!

1 (14-ounce) jar marinated artichoke hearts
2 cups freshly grated Parmesan cheese
2 cups mayonnaise
1 (4-ounce) can diced green chiles
1 to 1^1/$_2$ cups cubed cooked chicken

Thoroughly drain artichokes (there is a lot of oil). Cut into smaller pieces. Combine all the ingredients in medium saucepan; mix well. Cook over low heat until heated through. Do not let boil or the mixture will have a curdled look. Serve with crackers or French bread slices. Will serve perhaps 6 to 8 people.

TIP: It is hard to judge how many this will serve. It looks like a lot, but it will disappear very fast.

Cook's Tip

A fun way to serve Artichoke Dip with Chicken is in a bread bowl. Purchase a large round whole loaf of Italian or sourdough bread. Remove bread from center of loaf, leaving a 1-inch shell. Fill with hot dip. Serve with crackers or cut scooped out bread into medium cubes and use for dipping.

RUMAKI

MARINATE
OVEN

An old favorite.

> **¹/₂ pound chicken livers, cut in thirds**
> **¹/₄ cup soy sauce**
> **1 small garlic clove, minced**
> **1 (8-ounce) can whole water chestnuts, cut in thirds**
> **15 bacon slices, cut in half crosswise**

Clean chicken livers and pat dry. Combine soy sauce and garlic in small mixing bowl. Add chicken livers; cover and marinate in refrigerator several hours or overnight. When ready to serve, wrap a piece of liver and a water chestnut with a slice of bacon. Secure with a toothpick. Place on rack in shallow baking pan; bake at 425° for 20 to 25 minutes or until liver is cooked through and bacon is crisp. Makes about 30 appetizers.

VARIATION: If desired, add 2 tablespoons brown sugar to soy sauce and garlic.

PARSLEY

Soups and Sandwiches

BASIC CREAM OF CHICKEN SOUP   TOP OF STOVE

$^1/_4$ **cup butter or margarine**
$^1/_4$ **cup flour**
2 cups half-and-half
2 cups chicken broth
2 cups diced cooked chicken

Melt butter or margarine in medium saucepan. Stir in flour; cook, stirring frequently, about 3 to 4 minutes. Reduce heat; add half-and-half and broth, stirring until smooth. Cook until slightly thickened, stirring occasionally. Add chicken and cook 2 to 3 minutes. Makes 4 servings.
TIP: This is an excellent basic cream soup. For variety add:

> Sauteed mushrooms
> Cooked peas, corn or carrots
> Chopped cooked onion or celery

As you can see, this would be a good way to use those leftovers in the refrigerator.

CHICKEN CORN CHOWDER   TOP OF STOVE

$^1/_2$ **cup finely chopped onion**
1 cup cubed cooked chicken
1 (17-ounce) and 1 ($8^1/_2$-ounce) can creamed corn
3 cups milk
Salt and pepper to taste
$1^1/_2$ cups (6-ounces) grated Cheddar cheese

Add chopped onion and $^1/_2$ cup water to large heavy saucepan. Cook until onion is tender. Pour off water. Add remaining ingredients except cheese. Bring to a boil. Reduce heat; stir in a small amount of cheese at a time, stirring until cheese is melted. Makes about 6 cups.

TIP: After adding cheese, do not let the mixture boil or cheese will curdle.

CHICKEN RICE SOUP   TOP OF STOVE

> 2 tablespoons butter or margarine
> 4 tablespoons flour
> 4 cups chicken broth
> 2 cups cubed cooked chicken
> 2 cups cooked long-grain rice
> $^1/_2$ cup whipping cream

Melt butter in large deep pot or saucepan. Add flour; stir until well blended. Cook until bubbles form, stirring constantly. Add 2 cups chicken broth; stir until smooth. Stir in remaining broth. Cook until slightly thickened. Add chicken and rice; bring to a boil. Reduce heat and stir in cream. Heat until hot, but not boiling. Makes 6 servings.

TIP: If you do not have a well-seasoned chicken broth, you may have to add a little salt and pepper for more flavor.

CHICKEN RICE & WATER CHESTNUT SOUP   TOP OF STOVE

A quick tasty soup.

> 4 cups chicken broth
> $^3/_4$ cup finely cubed cooked chicken
> 1 cup cooked rice
> $^1/_2$ cup sliced water chestnuts, quartered
> $^1/_2$ cup frozen peas

In medium saucepan, heat chicken broth to a gentle boil. Reduce heat and add remaining ingredients. Simmer about 6 minutes to heat through. Makes 4 servings.

TIP: If using a well-seasoned chicken broth, you should not have to add any salt or pepper to this recipe.

SPLIT PEA SOUP WITH CHICKEN

TOP OF STOVE

    2 cups cubed cooked chicken
    8 cups chicken broth
    1 (16-ounce) package dried green split peas
    2 carrots, cut into small cubes
    1 cup chopped onion
    Salt and pepper to taste

Combine all the ingredients in a large pot or Dutch oven. Bring to a boil, reduce heat and simmer 60 minutes or until peas are tender, stirring occasionally. Makes 8 servings.

CREAM OF MUSHROOM SOUP

TOP OF STOVE

A wonderful first course soup for an extra special dinner.

    2 tablespoons, plus $^1/_2$ cup butter
    $^1/_2$ cup finely chopped onion
    4 ounces fresh mushrooms, chopped fine
    $^1/_4$ cup flour
    2 cups half-and-half
    2 cups rich chicken broth

Melt the 2 tablespoons butter in large saucepan. Add onion and cook until soft. Add chopped mushrooms and cook until mushrooms start to turn dark (do not overcook). Remove mixture and set aside. Melt the $^1/_2$ cup butter in same pan. Add flour; stir until smooth. Cook, over low heat, about 2 minutes, stirring constantly. Add half-and-half and cook until thickened, stirring frequently. Add chicken broth and bring to a boil. If soup is thicker than desired, add a little more broth. Makes 4 to 6 servings.

EGG FLOWER SOUP   TOP OF STOVE

A light refreshing soup.

>   6 cups chicken broth
>   2 tablespoons cornstarch
>   1 cup diced cooked chicken
> $1/2$ cup cooked green peas
>   2 eggs, slightly beaten
>   Salt and pepper to taste

In a large saucepan, bring chicken broth to a boil. Combine cornstarch with 4 tablespoons water. Add to broth, stirring until slightly thickened. Add chicken and peas. Slowly pour in eggs; gently stir just once or twice. Add salt and pepper to taste. Remove from heat and serve. Makes 4 to 6 servings.

FRENCH ONION SOUP   TOP OF STOVE
                                                      BROIL
A well seasoned chicken broth makes a very tasty onion soup.

>   4 medium onions
>   2 tablespoons flour
>   8 cups chicken broth
>   Salt and white pepper
>   French bread
>   Grated Swiss or Mozzarella cheese

Slice onions. You should have about 8 cups. Separate into rings. Put $1/4$ cup water in large heavy pot or Dutch oven. Add onions and cook until soft. Sprinkle flour over onions; stir to mix. Add chicken broth. Add salt and pepper to taste. Bring to a boil. Reduce heat; cover and simmer about 20 minutes. Taste again for seasoning. Meanwhile, slice bread into 1-inch thick slices. Toast on both sides. Ladle soup into individual or one large oven-proof bowl. Cut toast into bite-size cubes and sprinkle over soup. Sprinkle generously with cheese, covering all of the bread. Place under broiler and broil until cheese is bubbly and just starting to brown. Makes 6 servings.

TIP: To avoid tearing vapors from onions, chill before slicing.

LOW-CAL CHICKEN VEGETABLE SOUP   TOP OF STOVE

1¹/₂ cups chopped onion
2 (10³/₄-ounce) cans condensed chicken broth
2 (28-ounce) cans whole tomatoes, cut up
2 cups sliced carrots
4 cups thinly sliced cabbage
3 to 4 cups cubed cooked chicken

Combine first 3 ingredients in large pot. Add 2 cups water; cook 20 minutes. Add carrots and cabbage and cook 1 hour. Add chicken last 10 minutes of cooking time. Makes about 8 servings at 200 calories each.

TIP: If salt is permitted in your diet and the chicken broth doesn't add enough flavor, you may wish to add salt to taste. Sprinkling a little grated Parmesan over your bowl of soup will also add a lot of flavor and not a lot of calories.

ORIENTAL CHICKEN NOODLE SOUP   TOP OF STOVE

1¹/₂ cups cubed cooked chicken
1 (3-ounce) package chicken flavored Oriental Noodles
4 cups chicken broth
1 (10-ounce) package frozen mixed vegetables
¹/₃ cup thinly sliced celery
2 tablespoons soy sauce

In a large saucepan, break up the noodles. Add the seasoning packet, broth, vegetables, celery and soy sauce. Add 1 cup water. Bring mixture to a boil. Add chicken. Reduce heat; simmer about 5 minutes or until vegetables are tender. (Do not overcook.) Makes 4 to 6 servings.

POTATO CHICKEN CHOWDER

TOP OF STOVE

2 cups diced potatoes
3/4 cup chopped onion
1 1/2 cups cubed cooked chicken
1 (16-ounce) can creamed corn
3 cups milk
Salt and pepper to taste

In large saucepan, cover potatoes and onion with water and cook until potatoes are done. Pour off water. Add chicken, corn and milk. Add salt and pepper to taste. Makes 6 servings.

TIP: If you want a Cream Chowder, combine 1 tablespoon cornstarch with 2 tablespoons cold water. Stir into soup and cook until slightly thickened.

PUMPKIN SOUP

TOP OF STOVE

A quick and easy soup. Most people either really like pumpkin soup or they can take it or leave it.

1/2 cup butter
1 (16-ounce) can pumpkin
1 cup chicken broth
2 cups half-and-half
Salt and pepper to taste
Sour cream (optional)

Melt butter in a large heavy saucepan. Stir in pumpkin, broth and half-and-half until blended. On low heat, heat through, but do not boil. Add salt and pepper to taste. Serve in soup bowls; garnish center with a small dollop of sour cream. Makes 4 to 6 servings.

VEGETABLE CHICKEN SOUP

TOP OF STOVE

A nice way to use leftover chicken and get your vegetables for the day.

> **2 cups cubed cooked chicken**
> **1 cup chopped onion**
> **2^1/$_2$ cups cubed potatoes**
> **2 large carrots, sliced**
> **1 (1 pound 12-ounce) can tomatoes, cut up, undrained**
> **Salt and pepper to taste**

Combine all the ingredients in a large pot or Dutch oven. Add about 4 cups water. Cook, over medium-low heat, 1 hour or until vegetables are tender. Add salt and pepper to taste. Makes about 6 servings.

TIP: This recipe doesn't have a lot of color, so if you have any leftover peas, you may want to add those to the pot.

CHICKEN BROTH

TOP OF STOVE

Homemade chicken broth that has simmered 2 to 3 hours will produce a much richer broth than that purchased in a can. Broth can be made ahead and frozen for using in soups, sauces and main dishes. To make your own use:

> **4 to 5 pounds chicken backs and wings**
> **2 large onions, quartered, separated**
> **3 carrots, sliced**
> **3 celery stalks, cut into 2-inch pieces**
> **Salt and pepper to taste**

Place ingredients in a large pot. Add water to cover. Bring to a boil; skim off foam that forms on the top. Simmer, partially covered, 2 to 3 hours. Remove chicken and vegetables. Strain broth. Taste for seasoning. Refrigerate until cool. Lift off fat that congeals on top. Broth is now ready to use or freeze.

AVOCADO AND CHICKEN SANDWICH

BROIL

A delicious open-faced sandwich.

> **4 slices whole wheat or rye bread, toasted**
> **Mayonnaise**
> **4 to 8 slices cooked chicken, depending on size**
> **4 slices bacon, cut in half, cooked**
> **1 avocado, thinly sliced**
> **4 slices Swiss cheese**

Spread desired amount of mayonnaise on each slice of bread. Top each with chicken slices, 2 slices cooked bacon, some avocado, and a slice of cheese. Place on baking sheet and broil, about 4 inches from the heat, just until cheese is melted. Makes 4 sandwiches.

BARBECUE CHICKEN SANDWICH

These can become an addiction.

> **Thinly sliced cooked chicken breast, about 2 to 3 slices per sandwich**
> **$1/2$ cup bottled barbecue sauce**
> **Hot pepper sauce (like Tabasco)**
> **1 cup shredded cabbage**
> **4 hamburger buns**

Combine barbecue sauce with 2 to 3 drops hot pepper sauce (or to taste). Spread desired amount of sauce on buns. Top with thinly sliced chicken and some of the shredded cabbage. Makes 4 sandwiches.

TIP: I have tried different barbecue sauces with this recipe and my favorite is Kraft's Regular Barbecue Sauce with a small amount of the hot pepper sauce added. This is equally as delicious using cooked and thinly sliced roast pork.

CHICKEN CROISSANT SANDWICH

The first three ingredients are used to make a cream cheese spread. Use this spread on desired number of sandwiches - there should be enough to make 6 to 8 sandwiches depending on the size of the croissants.

>   1 (8-ounce) package cream cheese, softened
> $^1/_2$ cup finely chopped walnuts or pecans
> $^1/_4$ cup orange marmalade or apricot preserves
>   Croissants
>   Thin slices of cooked chicken
>   Lettuce leaves

Combine first three ingredients; mix well. Spread on top and bottom halves of croissants. On bottom halves, place a layer of chicken slices. Add lettuce leaves and croissant tops.

TIP: The cream cheese spread is also very good on hot muffins right out of the oven.

VARIATION: Omit spread; butter croissants. Add thin slices of cranberry sauce or spoon on a thin layer of whole cranberry sauce.

CHICKEN PROVOLONE SANDWICH

>   For each Sandwich:
>   Sourdough roll
>   Butter or margarine, softened
>   Thinly sliced cooked chicken
>   Slice of provolone cheese
>   Thinly sliced tomato
>   Alfalfa sprouts

Split rolls; spread with softened butter or margarine. Layer with slices of chicken, cheese and tomato. Top with alfalfa sprouts.

TORTILLA-CHICKEN SANDWICH

If you are tired of the same old soup and sandwich lunch, try this delightful combination of thinly sliced deli chicken (or turkey) and flour tortillas.

For each sandwich:
Mayonnaise
8-inch flour tortilla
2 pieces thinly sliced deli chicken or turkey
1 thin slice American or Havarti cheese
Shredded lettuce

Spread a thin layer of mayonnaise on tortilla. Top with sliced chicken and cheese. Sprinkle shredded lettuce over top. Roll up to enclose filling. Cut in half to serve.

TIP: Filling ingredients should not be too thick or the tortilla will be difficult to roll. If the tortilla is a little dry, it may tend to crack when rolling. If this should happen, wrap the tortilla in foil and warm slightly. If sliced cheese tends to be hard to roll, shred the cheese first and sprinkle over chicken.

Cook's Tip

Many mayonnaise type chicken salads can be used as a delicious filling for sandwiches. One of my favorite is to layer stacks of round bread slices with filling, then frost with softened cream cheese thinned slightly with milk. The "cake" can then be decorated as desired and cut into wedges to serve. Very attractive for a luncheon or light dinner.

Salads,
Dressings,
Stuffings,
&
Sauces

BANANA CHICKEN SALAD CHILL

 2 cups cubed cooked chicken
 $^3/_4$ cup thinly sliced celery
 1 orange (peeled and divided into segments)
 1 large banana, sliced
 $^1/_3$ cup peanuts
 $^2/_3$ cup mayonnaise

Combine first 5 ingredients in large mixing bowl. Toss gently with just enough mayonnaise to moisten. Cover and chill. Makes 4 servings.

TIP: If using canned mandarin oranges in place of the fresh orange, add last and gently mix into the salad.

CHICKEN AND APPLE SALAD CHILL

You will be pleasantly surprised at how cabbage and chicken combines to make this delicious salad.

 1 cup cubed cooked chicken
 2 cups shredded cabbage
 1 cup cubed Golden or Red Delicious apples, (do not peel)
 1 cup coarsely chopped pecans
 $^1/_3$ cup chopped celery
 $^3/_4$ cup mayonnaise

Combine first 5 ingredients in a large mixing bowl. Add just enough mayonnaise to moisten. Cover and chill at least 1 hour before serving. Makes 4 servings.

TIP: One (8-ounce) can crushed pineapple (drained) is also very good in this salad.

APPLE-CHEESE CHICKEN SALAD

CHILL

> 2 cups cubed cooked chicken
> 1/2 cup chopped celery
> 1/2 cup coarsely chopped walnuts
> 1 Red Delicious apple, chopped (do not peel)
> 1/2 cup Swiss or Cheddar cheese, cut into small cubes
> 3/4 cup mayonnaise

Combine first 5 ingredients in a large mixing bowl. Toss with just enough mayonnaise to moisten. Chill until ready to serve. Makes 4 to 6 servings.

CHICKEN MANDARIN SALAD

Use desired amounts of:
> Spinach, washed and stemmed
> Cubed cooked chicken
> Sliced fresh mushrooms
> Mandarin oranges
> Red onion, thinly sliced and separated into rings
> A Vinaigrette-type dressing

Combine first 5 ingredients. Toss with just enough dressing to lightly coat leaves.

CHICKEN SALAD BERNSTEIN

Quick and easy.

> 2 cups cubed cooked chicken
> 2 cups cooked broccoli flowerettes
> 1/3 cup sliced ripe olives
> 3 to 4 plum tomatoes, quartered
> Bernstein's Cheese Fantastico bottled dressing

Place first 4 ingredients in large mixing bowl. Toss with enough dressing to lightly coat. Makes 4 to 6 servings.

MACADAMIA CHICKEN SALAD   CHILL

Macadamia nuts are very expensive, but nice for a special occasion.

4 cups cooked cubed chicken
1 (20-ounce) can pineapple chunks, drained
1 cup Macadamia nuts, halved or cut into fourths
$^1/_2$ cup thinly sliced celery
$^1/_4$ teaspoon ground ginger
1 cup mayonnaise

In a large bowl, combine first 4 ingredients. Combine ginger and mayonnaise; mix well. Add just enough mayonnaise to salad to moisten. Cover and chill to blend flavors. Makes 4 to 6 servings.

TIP: To substitute, use cashews or pecan halves for the Macadamia nuts.

Cook's Tip

Leftover cooked chicken can be used for salads, soups and sandwiches.

For the most tender and attractive chicken salads, use the white meat only.

ORIENTAL CHICKEN SALAD

CHILL

    2 cups cubed cooked chicken
    $^3/_4$ cup cooked peas, drained
    $^1/_2$ cup thinly sliced celery
    $^1/_3$ cup finely chopped onion
    $^3/_4$ cup mayonnaise
    1 cup Chow Mein noodles

In large mixing bowl, combine first 4 ingredients. Add just enough mayonnaise to moisten. Cover and chill. When ready to serve, toss with Chow Mein noodles, adding additional mayonnaise if needed. Makes 4 servings.

TIP: If Chow Mein noodles are added too soon before serving, they will loose their delightful crunch.

PASTA-HERB CHICKEN SALAD

One of our local restaurants serves a delicious pasta salad with chicken. This recipe comes very close to the one they make.

    $1^1/_2$ to 2 cups cubed cooked chicken
    $2^1/_2$ cups cooked corkscrew shaped noodles
    1 head lettuce, torn into bite-size pieces
    $^1/_4$ cup grated carrots
    $^1/_2$ to $^3/_4$ cup sliced almonds
    Berstein's Creamy Herb & Garlic Italian Dressing

Combine first 5 ingredients in a large mixing bowl. Toss with just enough dressing to lightly coat leaves. Makes 4 to 6 servings.

PECAN CHICKEN SALAD

CHILL

Another recipe very close to a popular salad in one of our local restaurants.

2 cups cubed cooked chicken
$^1/_2$ cup pecan halves, broken in half
$^1/_3$ cup chopped celery
$^1/_2$ cup mayonnaise

Combine ingredients, adding just enough mayonnaise to moisten. Cover and chill until ready to serve. Makes 2 large or 3 small servings.

VARIATION: If desired, use equal parts mayonnaise and sour cream.

ROMAINE HAZELNUT SALAD

A nice luncheon salad.

1 head Romaine lettuce, torn into bite-size pieces.
$^1/_2$ cup cubed cooked chicken
8 slices bacon, cooked and crumbled
$^1/_2$ cup coarsely chopped hazelnuts
Dressing of your choice.

Combine first 4 ingredients in a large salad bowl. Toss with just enough dressing to lightly coat leaves. Makes 4 servings.

TIP: A poppy seed or Italian type dressing is very good on this salad.

SPINACH SALAD WITH CHICKEN

1 whole chicken breast, cooked and cubed
1 bunch fresh spinach
4 tablespoons sliced almonds
2 hard-cooked eggs, chopped
Your choice of bottled or homemade dressing

Combine first 4 ingredients in large salad bowl. Toss with just enough dressing to lightly coat leaves. Makes 4 servings.

VARIATION: If desired, add 4 ounces cubed Swiss, Mozzarella or Cheddar cheese. Sliced raw mushrooms may be added.

CHICKEN SALAD

CHILL

:ime favorite.

3 cups cubed cooked chicken
$^1/_3$ cup chopped celery
$^3/_4$ cup coarsely chopped apples (do not peel)
$^1/_3$ cup chopped walnuts
$^1/_2$ cup mayonnaise

In large mixing bowl, combine first 4 ingredients. Stir in just enough mayonnaise to moisten. Cover and chill until ready to serve. Makes 4 to 6 servings.

CHINESE CHICKEN SALAD

A nice and very filling luncheon salad.

2 cups cubed cooked chicken
1 medium head lettuce, shredded
$^1/_3$ cup sliced almonds
1 cup Chow Mein noodles
Dressing of your choice

Combine the first 4 ingredients in a large salad bowl. Toss with just enough dressing to lightly coat. Makes 4 large servings.

TIP: This salad is delicious with a number of different salad dressings, but the one I like best is Favorite Salad Dressing, page 43.

VARIATION: About 2 ounces of rice sticks can be substituted for the Chow Mein noodles. Make sure the oil is hot enough (375° to 400°) or they will not puff up the way they should.

CREAMY CHICKEN SALAD DRESSING

Makes a nice dressing for almost any chunky style chicken salad.

$^2/_3$ **cup mayonnaise**
$^1/_3$ **cup sour cream**
1 teaspoon lemon juice
$^1/_2$ **teaspoon salt**
$^1/_4$ **teaspoon ground black pepper**

In small bowl, combine all ingredients and mix well. Makes 1 cup.

VARIATION: Add about $^1/_2$ teaspoon dried dill weed to make a nice dip for fresh vegetables.

CREAMY MUSTARD DRESSING

A versatile dressing for chicken salads as well as tossed green salads.

$^1/_4$ **cup Dijon mustard**
$^1/_4$ **cup tarragon flavored wine vinegar**
$^3/_4$ **teaspoon dried dill weed**
1 cup oil
1 tablespoon half-and-half
1 tablespoon grated Parmesan cheese

Combine mustard, vinegar and dill weed. Slowly add oil, whisking after each addition until blended. Stir in half-and-half and Parmesan cheese. Makes 1$^1/_2$ cups.

CURRY MAYONNAISE DRESSING

A nice dressing with a wonderful curry flavor. Use with chicken and chicken and rice salads.

> 1 tablespoon white wine vinegar
> 1 egg
> 1 teaspoon salt
> 1^1/$_2$ teaspoons curry powder
> 1 cup oil
> ^{1}/$_2$ cup sour cream

Add first 4 ingredients to bowl of food processor or blender. Cover. Turn machine on and very slowly add oil through the top. When thick, turn off machine. Add sour cream. Pulse on and off until smooth and blended. Makes 1^3/$_4$ cups.

DIJON MUSTARD DRESSING   CHILL

It is always nice to have a versatile dressing on hand to use with almost all types of green salads. This recipe will keep at least a month in the refrigerator.

> 1 cup olive oil
> ^{1}/$_3$ cup red wine or garlic vinegar
> 3 tablespoons Dijon mustard
> 1 tablespoon mild-flavored honey
> ^{3}/$_4$ teaspoon salt
> 2 tablespoons finely chopped onion

Combine all the ingredients in a medium mixing bowl. Beat with hand or rotary mixer until thoroughly blended. Store in covered jar in refrigerator. Makes about 1^3/$_4$ cups.

ITALIAN STYLE DRESSING

An excellent dressing to use on most chicken pasta salads, chicken and rice salads, and chicken salads with spinach.

1 cup olive oil
$^1/_4$ cup red wine vinegar
1 teaspoon lemon juice
1 egg
1 teaspoon salt
1 tablespoon sugar

Combine ingredients in mixer bowl. Beat until smooth and well mixed. Makes 1$^1/_2$ cups.

MUSTARD DRESSING

TOP OF STOVE
CHILL

Excellent on chicken salads with spinach.

2 eggs
2 tablespoons dry mustard
$^1/_4$ cup sugar
1 teaspoon salt
$^1/_3$ cup white wine vinegar
1 cup whipping cream, divided

In medium saucepan, beat eggs with a hand mixer until smooth. Add mustard, sugar and salt; beat until well mixed. Add vinegar. Slowly add $^1/_2$ cup of the cream, stirring constantly. Cook over low heat until thickened. Remove from heat and add remaining cream, stirring to mix well. Cover and chill overnight. Serve at room temperature. Makes 1$^3/_4$ cups.

ORIENTAL SALAD DRESSING

A sweet oriental flavored dressing that is good on most chicken and spinach type salads.

   $^1/_2$ **cup oil**
   6 tablespoons rice vinegar or white vinegar
   2 teaspoons soy sauce
   $^1/_4$ **cup sugar**
   $^1/_2$ **teaspoon salt**

Combine all the ingredients. Mix well to dissolve the sugar. Makes about $^3/_4$ cup.

TIP: Recipe can be made ahead. Rice vinegar can usually be found in the oriental department of most supermarkets.

POPPY SEED DRESSING   CHILL

A popular dressing for chicken spinach salads as well as fruit salads.

   $^1/_2$ **cup oil**
   3 tablespoons apple cider vinegar
   6 tablespoons sugar
   $^1/_2$ **teaspoon salt**
   $^1/_2$ **teaspoon dry mustard**
   1 tablespoon poppy seeds

In mixer bowl, at low speed, mix the first 5 ingredients. Beat until blended and thickened. Stir in poppy seeds. Cover and chill at least 2 hours to blend flavors. Makes about 1 cup.

TIP: Will keep several days in the refrigerator.

QUICK CURRY DRESSING

A delicate flavored curry dressing. Use on rice or chicken pasta

$^1/_4$ **cup mayonnaise**
$^1/_4$ **cup sour cream**
$^1/_4$ **teaspoon curry powder (or to taste)**

Combine all the ingredients and mix well. Makes $^1/_2$ cup.

SWEET ONION DRESSING   CHILL

Especially good on spinach salads. Will keep several days in the refrigerator.

$^1/_2$ **cup olive oil**
$^1/_4$ **cup cider vinegar**
$^1/_4$ **cup finely chopped onion**
$^1/_2$ **teaspoon prepared mustard**
$^1/_2$ **teaspoon salt**
2 tablespoons sugar

Combine all the ingredients; mix well to blend. Chill until ready to serve. Makes about 1 cup.

FAVORITE SALAD DRESSING

When dieting, I like to use this dressing (just a little bit) on a large salad. You get a lot of flavor with just a few ingredients.

$^1/_4$ **cup oil**
3 tablespoons rice vinegar
$^1/_2$ **teaspoon salt**
$^1/_8$ **teaspoon pepper**
Artificial sweetener to equal 2 tablespoons sugar

Combine ingredients and mix thoroughly. Makes about $^1/_2$ cup.

TIP: One of my favorite salads is this dressing tossed with shredded lettuce, cooked cubed chicken and a sprinkle of Chow Mein noodles.

CORNBREAD STUFFING

TOP OF STOVE

Makes enough stuffing for one large roasting chicken.

> $^1/_4$ **cup butter**
> $^1/_2$ **cup chopped onion**
> $^1/_2$ **cup chopped celery**
> $^1/_2$ **teaspoon sage**
> **2 cups cornbread stuffing mix**
> $^1/_2$ **cup chopped pecans or walnuts**

Heat butter in small skillet; add onion and celery and cook until tender but not brown. Toss with remaining ingredients. Add about $^1/_2$ cup water or enough to slightly soften stuffing mixture.

LONG GRAIN & WILD RICE STUFFING

TOP OF STOVE

Can be used as a stuffing or a rice dish.

> **1 tablespoon butter or margarine**
> $^1/_3$ **cup sliced green onions (green part also)**
> **1 (6-ounce) package Long Grain & Wild Rice with seasoning packet**
> $^1/_2$ **cup chopped pecans, walnuts or cashews**

Heat butter in medium saucepan. Cook onions until soft but not browned. Stir in rice and seasoning packet. Add water as specified on package and cook according to directions. Stir in nuts. Makes enough stuffing for one large roasting chicken or 6 servings.

SAGE

MUSHROOM RICE STUFFING   TOP OF STOVE

This is a very good stuffing for a large roasting chicken or a small turkey.

 $^2/_3$ **cup slivered almonds**
 6 tablespoons butter or margarine, divided
 3 cups (about 8-ounces) fresh sliced mushrooms
 $^1/_2$ **cup chopped onion**
 $^1/_2$ **teaspoon salt (can omit)**
 2 cups cooked rice

Lightly brown almonds in 3 tablespoons of the butter or margarine. Remove almonds with a slotted spoon. Add remaining butter or margarine to skillet and sauté mushrooms and onion. Pour off excess butter. Toss with salt and rice.

VARIATION: You can also put the dressing in a casserole dish and top with chicken breasts (baste chicken with butter while baking) and bake at 350° for 60 minutes. Also, if you used salt when cooking the rice you may not need the salt in the recipe.

RICE AND APPLE STUFFING   TOP OF STOVE

Just a touch of curry makes this stuffing just right.

 $2^1/_2$ **cups cooked rice**
 4 strips bacon
 1 cup finely chopped onion
 1 teaspoon curry powder
 1 cup (coarsely torn) bread crumbs
 $^1/_2$ **cup chopped apple**

While rice is cooking, chop bacon and cook until crisp. Remove bacon and set aside. Add onion and curry powder to skillet; mix well. Cook onion until tender, but not brown. Combine onion with bacon, rice, bread crumbs and apple. Use to stuff one large roast chicken or four Cornish hens.

SAUSAGE BREAD STUFFING   TOP OF STOVE

This recipe makes enough stuffing for a large roasting chicken or capon with enough left to bake in a small casserole. It is also enough to stuff a 12 pound turkey.

  $^3/_4$ **pound bulk sausage**
  $^1/_2$ **cup butter or margarine**
  1$^1/_4$ cups coarsely chopped onion
  $^3/_4$ **cup chopped celery**
  1 (8-ounce) package herb seasoned bread stuffing mix
  1 cup chicken broth

Brown sausage in large skillet. Drain off fat; place sausage in a large mixing bowl. Melt butter or margarine in the skillet. Add onion and celery; cook until soft but not brown. Combine onion mixture with sausage and stuffing mix. Pour broth over top and gently mix until well coated. Use to stuff poultry or bake in a casserole.

VARIATION: For a nice change you could add raisins, chopped apple, or coarsely chopped pecans.

WILD RICE AND PECAN STUFFING   TOP OF STOVE

Makes enough stuffing for one roast chicken or 4 Cornish hens.

  1 (6-ounce) package white and wild rice
  1$^1/_2$ teaspoons fresh grated orange peel
  $^1/_3$ **cup chopped pecans**

Cook rice according to directions on package. Combine 2 cups of the rice mixture with the orange peel and pecans. Stuff chicken or Cornish hens.

BARBECUE SAUCE   TOP OF STOVE

This sauce will keep several days in the refrigerator.

$^3/_4$ cup catsup
$^1/_2$ cup butter or margarine
$^1/_4$ cup white vinegar
$^3/_4$ cup firmly packed light brown sugar
4 teaspoons chili powder
4 teaspoons Worcestershire sauce

Combine ingredients in medium saucepan; mix well. Bring to a boil and remove from heat. Makes 2 cups.

LIGHT BARBECUE SAUCE

A good barbecue sauce doesn't have to include tomatoes or tomato sauce.

$^1/_2$ cup plus 2 tablespoons pineapple juice
2 tablespoons oil
2 tablespoons white vinegar
2 tablespoons soy sauce
$1^1/_2$ teaspoons sugar
$^1/_2$ teaspoon ground ginger

Combine ingredients and mix well. Oil has a tendency to separate; stir to mix before each use. Makes 1 cup.

JUDY'S FAVORITE BARBECUE SAUCE   TOP OF STOVE

Made from ingredients you normally have on hand.

1 cup catsup
$^1/_3$ cup white vinegar
1 tablespoon light brown sugar
$^3/_4$ teaspoon black pepper
$1^1/_2$ teaspoons paprika
$^3/_4$ teaspoon garlic powder

Combine ingredients in medium saucepan. Bring to a boil, stirring occasionally; remove from heat. Makes $1^1/_2$ cups.

TIP: A nice barbecue sauce for chicken, ribs and pork chops.

HAWAIIAN BARBECUE SAUCE   TOP OF STOVE

This is a wonderful barbecue sauce, but the chicken must be browned first or the skin will be too soft.

$^1/_2$ cup firmly packed light brown sugar
$^1/_2$ cup catsup
$^1/_4$ cup prune juice
$^1/_4$ cup pineapple juice
1 teaspoon salt
1 garlic clove, minced

Combine ingredients in small saucepan. Bring to a boil, reduce heat and simmer 15 minutes. Makes about 1 cup.

TIP: This sauce is also delicious on ribs and pork chops.

QUICK BARBECUE SAUCE

I have a hard time using up a whole bottle of chili sauce; this recipe helps.

$^3/_4$ cup chili sauce
2 tablespoons soy sauce
2 tablespoons honey
$^3/_4$ teaspoon dry mustard
$^1/_2$ teaspoon prepared horseradish
$^1/_4$ teaspoon Tabasco sauce

Combine ingredients in small mixing bowl; mix well. Makes 1 cup.

TIP: When ready to use sauce, pour over chicken and bake at 375° for 60 minutes. Do not baste chicken while baking. This recipe is much better if you remove the skin from the chicken pieces.

SPICY BARBECUE SAUCE   TOP OF STOVE

$^1/_2$ **cup oil**
$^1/_2$ **cup fresh lemon juice**
2 tablespoons Worcestershire sauce
1$^1/_2$ teaspoons Tabasco sauce
2 tablespoons prepared mustard
$^1/_4$ **cup firmly packed light brown sugar**

Combine ingredients in a saucepan. Bring to a boil; remove from heat. Makes about 1$^1/_2$ cups.

SWEET-SOUR BARBECUE SAUCE   TOP OF STOVE

A sauce you will want to make often.

1 cup catsup
$^3/_4$ **cup white vinegar**
1$^1/_2$ teaspoons prepared mustard
1$^1/_2$ cups firmly packed light brown sugar

Combine ingredients in a small heavy saucepan. Bring to a boil; reduce heat and simmer 30 minutes. Makes about 2$^1/_2$ cups sauce.

TIP: Leftover sauce can be frozen. Use on chicken, ribs, steak, etc.

YEAR-ROUND BBQ SAUCE   TOP OF STOVE

A favorite barbecue sauce to keep on hand.

1 cup catsup
1 cup white vinegar
$^1/_2$ **cup firmly packed light brown sugar**
1$^1/_2$ teaspoons chili powder
$^1/_2$ **teaspoon salt**
1 teaspoon black pepper

Combine ingredients in medium saucepan; bring to a boil. Lower heat and simmer 40 minutes. Makes 2$^1/_2$ cups.

TIP: With today's choice of barbecue grills we can enjoy barbecuing year `round. Use the grill in a protected or covered area (not an enclosed area). If the weather is nasty, close the hood and check the food frequently.

GRAND MARNIER BASTING SAUCE

An easy, flavorful basting sauce for roasting chicken and Cornish hens.

> $^1/_2$ **cup melted butter or margarine**
> **3 tablespoons Grand Marnier liqueur**

Combine butter or margarine and liqueur. Use as a basting sauce when roasting chicken or baking whole Cornish hens. Makes about $^3/_4$ cup sauce.

VARIATION: Add $^1/_4$ teaspoon paprika.

MARMALADE BASTING SAUCE   TOP OF STOVE

Use this wonderful sauce to baste chicken and Cornish hens.

> $^3/_4$ **cup orange marmalade**
> **2 tablespoons Grand Marnier liqueur**
> **8 whole cloves**

In small sauce pan, combine ingredients and heat just until hot. Brush sauce on chicken, basting frequently until done.

ORANGE APRICOT SAUCE

Use as a basting sauce for roasting chicken and Cornish hens.

> $^3/_4$ **cup apricot preserves**
> **2 tablespoons orange juice**

Combine ingredients in small bowl; mix well. Use to baste poultry during last $^1/_2$ hour of cooking time, basting frequently. Makes $^3/_4$ cup.

SWEET-SOUR SAUCE   TOP OF STOVE

This is a wonderful sauce for Chicken Nuggets or Fried Chicken Strips (see index).

> 1 (6-ounce) can pineapple juice
> $^1/_4$ cup apple cider vinegar
> $^1/_4$ cup firmly packed light brown sugar
> 1 tablespoon cornstarch

Combine ingredients in a small saucepan. Mix well to dissolve the brown sugar and cornstarch. Cook over medium heat until mixture thickens, stirring frequently with a whisk. Makes $^3/_4$ cup.

QUICK TERIYAKI SAUCE   TOP OF STOVE

Serve as a dip for Chicken Nuggets.

> $^1/_2$ cup bottled teriyaki sauce
> $^1/_3$ cup apricot preserves
> 2 small garlic cloves, minced
> 3 small slices fresh ginger
> 1 tablespoon cornstarch

Combine first four ingredients in small saucepan. Bring to a boil. Combine cornstarch with $^1/_4$ cup water, stirring until smooth. Reduce heat; add cornstarch mixture to sauce. Cook over low heat until mixture thickens, stirring frequently. Makes about $^3/_4$ cup.

Cook's Tip

If using a barbecue sauce with a high sugar content, brush on chicken during last 15 minutes of cooking time. You can also pre-cook the chicken in the oven, 350° for about 45 minutes, basting with a vinaigrette dressing. When ready to serve, place on grill and brush with sauce. Cook until nicely glazed and tender.

FRESH TOMATO SAUCE   TOP OF STOVE

This is a very good made-from-scratch tomato sauce that can be served over poached or baked chicken breasts.

> ¹/₄ cup olive oil
> 2 large garlic cloves, minced
> 10 to 12 medium large tomatoes, peeled, seeded, coarsely chopped
> 1 teaspoon dried basil
> Salt and pepper to taste

Heat olive oil in 10-inch skillet. Add minced garlic and sauté 1 minute. Add tomatoes and cook, over low heat, until tomatoes soften. Add basil, salt and pepper. (The amount of salt will depend a lot on the quality of the tomatoes.) Cook until sauce thickens slightly and some of the liquid is reduced. Makes 4 cups.

VARIATION: Serve sauce over hot cooked spaghetti and sprinkle with grated Parmesan cheese.

RICH CREAM SAUCE   TOP OF STOVE

A creamy rich-tasting sauce to serve over chicken breasts.

> 2 tablespoons butter
> 2 teaspoons finely chopped shallots (or mild onion)
> 1 tablespoon Dijon mustard
> 4 tablespoons white wine
> 1 pint whipping cream
> Salt and pepper

In heavy medium saucepan, heat the butter. Add shallots; sauté about 2 minutes. Stir in mustard and wine; cook 3 to 4 minutes. Add cream and just a dash of salt and pepper. Cook over low heat until sauce thickens and is reduced. This may take as long as 30 minutes. Watch carefully and stir sauce occasionally. Pour over chicken and serve. Makes about 1¹/₂ cups sauce.

VARIATION: Add sautéed mushrooms and toss with hot fettucini noodles or toss with noodles and small strips of cooked chicken breast; sprinkle with grated Parmesan cheese.

MORNAY SAUCE

TOP OF STOVE

A delicious sauce served over cooked chicken slices. Also very good served over Easy Baked Fried Chicken (page 111).

> $^1/_4$ **cup butter or margarine**
> **3 tablespoons flour**
> $^3/_4$ **cup chicken broth**
> **1 cup cream or half-and-half**
> **2 egg yolks**
> $^1/_2$ **cup freshly grated Parmesan cheese, room temperature**

Melt butter in heavy medium saucepan over low heat. Add flour; stir until well mixed. Cook until mixture bubbles and is smooth. Combine chicken broth and cream; add to flour mixture, stirring constantly (with a whisk) until smooth. Cook 1 to 2 minutes or until slightly thickened. Remove from heat and stir 4 tablespoons of the sauce into the egg yolks. Add mixture to pan. Cook 2 to 3 minutes or until thickened. Add Parmesan cheese; stir until melted and smooth. Serve over chicken.

TIP: If sauce gets too thick, gradually stir in more chicken broth or cream.

SWISS SAUCE

TOP OF STOVE

A nice sauce to serve over sautéed chicken breasts and even some rice dishes.

> $^1/_4$ **cup butter or margarine**
> $^1/_4$ **cup flour**
> $2^1/_2$ **cups milk**
> $1^1/_2$ **cups (6-ounces) grated Swiss cheese**

In saucepan, melt butter over medium heat. When butter bubbles, quickly whisk in the flour until smooth. Cook 1 to 2 minutes. Remove from heat; add milk and stir until smooth. Return to heat; bring to a boil, stirring constantly. Reduce heat to low. Add grated cheese; stir until melted. At this point, do not let the cheese mixture get too hot or it will have a curdled look. Makes about 3 cups.

TIP: If desired, check for taste and see if you would like to add a little salt to the recipe.

CREAM GRAVY

TOP OF STOVE

4 tablespoons fat from frying chicken
4 tablespoons flour
2 cups milk
Salt and pepper

Leave 4 tablespoons fat in pan along with the crusty bits that stick to the bottom. Heat until hot. Stir in flour until blended. Cook until brown and bubbly, stirring constantly. Add milk; stir to mix well. Continue cooking, stirring frequently, until gravy is thickened, about 5 minutes. Add salt and pepper to taste. Makes 2 cups.

TIP: If gravy is too thick, stir in a little milk. If too thin, add a little flour mixed with a small amount of water.

CLARIFIED BUTTER

TOP OF STOVE

1 pound butter

Melt butter in small saucepan. Pour butter into glass measuring cup; let stand. Skim off foam. Carefully pour off butter and discard the milky sediment that accumulates on the bottom. Refrigerate and use as needed. Makes about 1¹/₂ cups.

TIP: Clarified butter will not burn as easily as plain butter. Use to sauté fish, chicken, chops, French toast, etc.

Main Dishes
and
Casseroles

WALNUT PARMESAN CHICKEN   TOP OF STOVE

A wonderful company recipe in less than 30 minutes.

4 chicken breast halves, skinned and boned
$1/2$ cup grated Parmesan cheese
$1/2$ cup flour
6 tablespoons finely ground walnuts
$1/2$ cup milk
6 tablespoons butter

Wash chicken and pat dry. Combine Parmesan cheese, flour and walnuts. Coat chicken pieces with crumb mixture; dip in milk, and coat again with crumb mixture. Heat butter in a large heavy skillet over medium heat. Add chicken and sauté, 3 to 4 minutes per side, until golden brown and chicken is cooked through. Do not cook too fast or chicken will brown too quickly on the outside and will not be cooked through. Makes 4 servings.

TIP: I would suggest using clarified butter, page 54, for this recipe. It will not burn as easily as regular butter.

ANNE'S BAKED CHICKEN   TOP OF STOVE
                                           OVEN

Preparation time is kept to a minimum.

4 chicken breast halves or 1 chicken, cut up
1 (10-ounce) jar currant jelly
$1/4$ cup packed light brown sugar
3 tablespoons orange or pineapple juice

Wash chicken and pat dry. Place, skin-side up, in greased 7x11-inch baking dish. Combine remaining ingredients in small saucepan. Heat until jelly is melted; mix well. Pour over chicken. Bake at 375° for 50 to 60 minutes, or until chicken is tender and richly glazed, basting frequently with the sauce. Makes 4 servings.

CHICKEN WITH MUSTARD SAUCE   TOP OF STOVE

Just the right blend of flavors.

>   4 to 6 chicken breast halves, skinned and boned
>   2 tablespoons butter or margarine
> $^1/_4$ cup finely chopped onion
>   1 cup white wine
>   1 cup whipping cream
> $^1/_3$ cup honey mustard or Dijon mustard

Lightly brown chicken in heated butter or margarine. Remove chicken. Add onion and cook until tender, adding additional butter if necessary. Return chicken to pan; add wine. Bring to a boil; reduce heat and simmer 10 minutes. Remove chicken and keep warm. Add cream and simmer 5 to 6 minutes. Stir in mustard and blend well. Cook 2 to 3 minutes. If sauce gets too thick, add a little more cream or some milk. Serve sauce with chicken or pour over chicken and serve. Makes 4 to 6 servings.

VEGETABLE AND CHICKEN DISH   TOP OF STOVE

A nice colorful vegetable main dish.

>   4 chicken breast halves
>   Salt and pepper
>   2 tablespoons oil
> $1^1/_4$ cups chicken broth
>   2 cups cut up broccoli
>   1 medium yellow squash, sliced

Sprinkle chicken with salt and pepper. Heat oil in large skillet; brown chicken on both sides. Add chicken broth; cover and cook 15 to 20 minutes or until chicken is cooked through. Add broccoli and squash; sprinkle with salt and pepper. Cover and cook 5 to 6 minutes or until vegetables are crisp tender. Makes 4 servings.

BAKED CHICKEN AND BISCUITS

An "easy on the budget" recipe.

1 chicken, cut up
³/₄ cup flour
Salt and pepper
¹/₄ cup butter or margarine
¹/₄ cup shortening
1 can refrigerator biscuits

Coat chicken with flour seasoned with salt and pepper. Place butter and shortening in shallow baking pan with a rim (like a jelly roll pan). Place in 425° oven to melt; stir to blend. Place chicken, skin-side down, in pan. Bake 45 minutes. Remove pan from oven; turn chicken and place at one end. Arrange biscuits in one layer at opposite end of pan. Bake 12 to 15 minutes or until biscuits are golden. Makes 4 servings.

Cook's Tip

Leftover chicken can be a great help in today's busy households. Cold chicken slices can be served on a platter along with an assortment of sliced meats, vegetables and cheese. A small amount of chicken can be combined with leftover ham in a casserole or salad. A little chicken goes a long way when added to your favorite soup recipes.

SMOTHERED CHICKEN

TOP OF STOVE
OVEN

An old-fashioned dish still popular today.

> 1 chicken, cut up
> 1/2 plus 1/3 cup flour
> 1 1/2 teaspoons salt
> 1/4 teaspoon pepper
> 4 tablespoons butter
> 1/2 cup finely chopped onion

Wash chicken and pat dry. Combine the 1/2 cup flour, salt and pepper. Roll chicken in flour mixture to coat. Heat butter in large heavy skillet. Brown chicken on all sides. Place chicken, skin-side up, in a 9x13-inch baking dish or roasting pan. Add onion to drippings in skillet; cook until soft. Add 1 1/2 cups water to skillet; bring to a boil. Pour over chicken. Cover tightly with a lid or foil. Bake at 350° for 60 minutes. Remove chicken and keep warm.

Carefully pour liquid from baking dish into skillet used for browning; bring to a boil. Combine the remaining 1/3 cup flour with 1 cup water; mix until smooth. Add to hot liquid. Cook, stirring constantly, until gravy thickens. Taste for seasoning. Makes 4 servings.

TIP: Gravy is delicious served over rice or mashed potatoes.

BAKED CHICKEN ROMANO

OVEN

A simple recipe with lots of flavor.

> 4 chicken breast halves, skin removed
> 1/3 cup flour
> 1/2 cup butter or margarine, melted
> 1/2 cup grated Romano cheese
> 1/2 cup white wine

Coat chicken with flour. Place, skin-side up, in 7x11-inch baking dish. Pour butter or margarine over chicken. Bake at 350° for 30 minutes, basting a couple of times. Sprinkle grated cheese evenly over chicken. Add wine. Bake 30 minutes, basting occasionally with butter mixture. Serve chicken with some of the sauce. Makes 4 servings.

TARRAGON CHICKEN AND CREAM   OVEN

Will fill your kitchen with the wonderful aroma of baked chicken and tarragon.

> **1 chicken, cut up**
> **³/₄ cup flour**
> **Salt and pepper**
> **1 cup heavy cream**
> **¹/₃ cup dry sherry**
> **Tarragon**

Wash chicken and pat dry. Combine flour, salt and pepper. Roll chicken in flour to coat both sides. Place, skin-side up, in greased 9x13-inch baking dish. Combine cream and sherry; pour over chicken. Sprinkle lightly with tarragon. Cover tightly and bake at 350° for 45 minutes. Uncover and bake 25 to 30 minutes or until chicken is lightly browned. Makes 4 servings.

TIP: Mixed herbs can be substituted for the tarragon. Serve with hot buttered noodles, Chinese pea pods with water chestnuts and sour-dough rolls.

BAKED CHICKEN WITH APRICOT GLAZE   OVEN

Easy on the cook.

> **4 to 6 chicken breast halves**
> **Salt and pepper**
> **Garlic powder**
> **¹/₃ cup butter or margarine, melted**
> **1 cup apricot preserves**

Wash chicken and pat dry. Sprinkle both sides lightly with salt, pepper and garlic powder. Place chicken, skin-side up, in shallow baking dish. Pour butter or margarine over top. Bake at 350° for 30 minutes. Stir apricot preserves to soften. Spoon over chicken. Bake 20 minutes or until chicken is richly glazed, basting frequently with the sauce.

TIP: If desired, remove skin on chicken before baking.

CHICKEN IN A POT   OVEN

This recipe is so tender and moist.

> **1 chicken, cup up**
> **Lemon pepper**
> **$^1/_4$ teaspoon paprika**
> **1 cup finely chopped onion**
> **$^1/_4$ cup butter or margarine**
> **$^1/_2$ cup white wine**

Sprinkle chicken with lemon pepper and paprika. Place, skin-side up, in a deep casserole or Dutch oven. Add onions. Dot with small pieces of butter or margarine. Cover and bake at 350° for 60 minutes. Add wine and bake for 30 minutes. Makes 4 servings.

TIP: This recipe has a wonderful flavor, but the chicken does not brown. For more color, serve garnished with parsley or fresh steamed vegetables.

BERNSTEIN'S BAKED CHICKEN   OVEN

I hope your supermarket carries Bernstein's dressings. They can be used in many chicken and meat recipes as well as your favorite salad combinations.

> **4 to 6 chicken breast halves, or 1 chicken, cut up**
> **Bernstein's Cheese Fantastico bottled dressing**

Brush both sides of chicken with dressing. Place, skin-side up, on baking sheet. Bake at 400° for 45 to 60 minutes or until tender and golden brown, brushing once or twice with additional dressing. Makes 4 to 6 servings.

TIP: If desired, remove skin from chicken.

GARLIC-BUTTER CHICKEN   OVEN

A quick and easy recipe for one of those days when you want to eat and run.

    1 chicken, cut up
    $1/2$ cup butter or margarine, melted
    1 tablespoon garlic salt
    $1/4$ teaspoon freshly ground black pepper.

Place chicken, skin-side down, in 9x13-inch pan. Combine remaining ingredients. Brush chicken with some of the butter mixture and bake at 350° for 30 minutes, basting a couple of times. Turn chicken, and bake another 30 minutes or until lightly browned, basting frequently. Makes 4 servings.

MAPLE SAUCE CHICKEN   OVEN

Easy on the cook.

    1 chicken, cut up
    1 large onion, sliced
    $1/2$ cup maple syrup
    $1/2$ cup ketchup
    $1/4$ cup white vinegar
    2 tablespoons Dijon mustard

Wash chicken and pat dry. Place onion slices in buttered 9x13-inch baking dish. Arrange chicken on top, skin-side up. Combine remaining ingredients; pour over top. Bake at 350° for 60 to 70 minutes or until nicely glazed, basting frequently with the sauce. Makes 4 servings.

QUICK BAKED CHICKEN   OVEN

    1 chicken, cut up
    $1/2$ cup Italian dressing
    $1^1/2$ cups crushed cornflakes

Wash chicken and pat dry. Dip in Italian dressing and roll in cornflake crumbs to coat. Place on greased baking sheet. Bake at 350° for 60 minutes or until tender. Makes 4 servings.

BROCCOLI-TOMATO CHICKEN   TOP OF STOVE

Stir-fry recipes are so quick, easy and kind to the budget.

    2 chicken breast halves, skinned and boned
    2 tablespoons oil, divided
    2 small onions, sliced and separated into rings
    2 cups cut up broccoli
    1 medium tomato, cut into wedges
    Salt and pepper

Cut chicken into bite-size chunks or strips. Toss chicken with 1 tablespoon of the oil. Place in large skillet. Cook over high heat, stirring frequently, until cooked through. Add remaining oil and onion slices. Cook over medium heat, about 2 minutes. Add broccoli and tomato. Sprinkle with salt and pepper. Cover and cook 4 to 6 minutes or until vegetables are crisp tender. Makes 4 servings.

VARIATION: Substitute sliced yellow squash or zucchini for the tomato.

STOVE-TOP HONEY CHICKEN   TOP OF STOVE

A nice honey flavor.

    6 to 8 chicken legs or thighs
    $1/2$ cup butter or margarine
    $1/2$ cup honey (a mild flavor is best)
    4 tablespoons fresh lemon juice
    $3/4$ teaspoon ground ginger

In large skillet, brown chicken on all sides in heated butter. Combine remaining ingredients; pour over chicken. Cover; reduce heat and simmer 30 minutes, basting occasionally. Uncover; turn chicken and cook 10 minutes, basting frequently. Makes 3 to 4 servings.

STUFFED CHICKEN ROLL-UPS   OVEN

A company favorite.

  4 large chicken breast halves, skinned and boned
  2 cups herb-seasoned bread stuffing mix
  2 eggs
  8 tablespoons butter, melted, divided
  $^1/_3$ cup coarsely chopped pecans
  $^3/_4$ cup flour

Place each chicken breast half on wax paper; pound lightly and evenly to about $^1/_4$-inch thickness. Combine stuffing mix, 1 egg, 3 tablespoons of the butter and pecans. If mixture is dry, add a little water to moisten. Top one end of each chicken breast with $^1/_4$th of the stuffing. Carefully fold other end over the stuffing, pressing to partially seal. Mix remaining egg with 1 tablespoon water; mix well. Coat chicken with flour, dip in egg, coat again in flour. Place on greased baking sheet. Pour remaining butter over top. Bake at 350° for 50 to 60 minutes or until chicken is tender and golden, basting frequently with the drippings. Makes 4 servings.

BUSY DAY CHICKEN   OVEN

For busy cooks, this will save the day.

  4 chicken breast halves, skin removed
  $^1/_2$ cup sour cream
  1 cup finely crushed Ritz crackers
  $^1/_2$ cup butter or margarine, melted

Brush both sides of chicken with sour cream. Roll in cracker crumbs to coat. Place chicken on baking sheet and drizzle butter over top. Bake at 375° for 45 minutes or until lightly browned and crisp. Makes 4 servings.

TIP: You can substitute plain yogurt for the sour cream.

CHEESE STUFFED CHICKEN BREASTS   OVEN

A little different taste treat. Very good.

> **4 to 6 chicken breast halves**
> **3 to 4 ounces German butter, Monterey Jack, or Swiss cheese, sliced**
> **Fresh or dried tarragon**
> **$^1/_4$ cup butter, melted**
> **$^2/_3$ cup green or red pepper jelly, melted**

Gently loosen the skin on each chicken breast, taking care not to tear or remove skin from the chicken. Sprinkle the cheese slices with a little tarragon. Stuff cheese under the skin. Secure with toothpicks to prevent cheese from running out. Place in greased baking dish, skin-side up. Pour melted butter over chicken. Bake at 350° for 15 minutes; pour melted jelly over top. Bake 30 to 40 minutes or until chicken is tender and glazed, basting frequently with the sauce. Makes 4 to 6 servings.

CHICKEN AND WINE   TOP OF STOVE

Simple, but tasty.

> **4 chicken breast halves or 1 chicken, quartered**
> **4 tablespoons butter or margarine**
> **1 cup chopped onion**
> **$^3/_4$ cup chopped celery**
> **$1^1/_2$ cups white wine**

Lightly brown chicken in heated butter or margarine in heavy skillet. Remove chicken. Add onion and celery to skillet; cook until tender but not brown. Stir in wine. Return chicken to skillet. Cover and cook for 1 hour, basting a couple of times with the sauce. Makes 4 servings.

STOVE TOP CHICKEN AND RICE

TOP OF STOVE

Easy to prepare.

> **4 chicken breast halves**
> **$1/4$ cup butter or margarine**
> **2 tablespoons flour**
> **2 cups chicken broth**
> **1 teaspoon garlic salt**
> **$3/4$ cup long-grain rice**

Melt butter or margarine in a deep heavy skillet, brown chicken pieces on both sides. Remove chicken and set aside. Add flour to butter in skillet; stir until smooth. Add chicken broth and garlic salt. Bring to a boil. Add chicken, skin-side up. Reduce heat, cover and simmer 10 minutes. Sprinkle rice between pieces of chicken, stirring to distribute more evenly, making sure all the rice is covered with liquid. Simmer, covered, 20 to 30 minutes or until most of the liquid is absorbed and rice is tender. Makes 4 servings.

CHICKEN AND MUSHROOMS IN CREAM

TOP OF STOVE

To quote my daughter, "Yummmm."

> **4 chicken breast halves, skinned and boned**
> **$1/3$ cup butter or margarine**
> **$1/2$ cup finely chopped onion**
> **3 cups sliced fresh mushrooms**
> **1 cup whipping cream**
> **$3/4$ cup freshly grated Parmesan cheese**

Cut chicken into bite-size chunks or strips. Sauté in heated butter 3 to 4 minutes. Add onion and mushrooms; cook 3 to 4 minutes, stirring occasionally. Add cream and cook over medium heat until slightly thickened. Lower heat; add grated cheese, stirring to blend. Cook over low heat until cheese is melted and sauce is smooth. (Do not cook too fast or sauce will separate.) Serve right away over rice or noodles. Makes 4 servings.

CHICKEN AND ONIONS   TOP OF STOVE

A lot of flavor with just a few ingredients

    1 chicken, cut up, skin removed
    4 tablespoons oil
    2 large onions, sliced, separated into rings
    1/4 cup chicken broth
    1 teaspoon salt
    1 teaspoon paprika

In large skillet, brown chicken in hot oil. To prevent chicken from sticking, cook over medium heat and turn frequently. Remove chicken. Add onions to skillet. Cook 5 to 6 minutes or until onions are just starting to get limp, stirring frequently. Stir in broth, salt and paprika. Return chicken to skillet; top with some of the onions. Cover; cook over low heat 30 minutes or until chicken is cooked through. Makes 4 servings.

CHICKEN AND PINEAPPLE   TOP OF STOVE
                                                        OVEN
Makes a tasty sauce.

    1 chicken, cut up
    1/2 cup flour
    Salt and pepper
    1/4 cup butter or margarine
    1 (20-ounce) can pineapple chunks, with juice

Wash chicken and pat dry. Combine flour, salt and pepper. Roll chicken in flour to coat. Cook chicken in melted butter, in heavy skillet, until browned on all sides. Place chicken, skin-side up, in greased 9x13-inch baking dish. Pour pineapple chunks and juice over chicken. Cover and bake at 350° for 45 minutes. Uncover and bake 30 minutes or until nicely browned (do not baste). Makes 4 servings.

TIP: Sauce is very good served over rice.

STOVE TOP CHICKEN   TOP OF STOVE

Simple ingredients are often the best.

>   1 chicken, cut in quarters
>   4 tablespoons butter or margarine, divided
>   1 garlic clove, minced
>   1 cup chopped onion
>   Salt and pepper to taste
>   2 tablespoons tomato paste

Melt 2 tablespoons butter in large deep skillet or Dutch oven. Add garlic and onion; cook until onion is soft, but not brown. Remove onion and set aside. Add remaining 2 tablespoons butter; brown chicken on both sides. Salt and pepper to taste. Combine tomato paste with cooked onion; add to skillet. Add 2 cups water. Cover and simmer 1½ hours or until chicken is tender. Serve sauce over chicken. Makes 4 servings.

TIP: The sauce is also delicious thickened with 2 tablespoons cornstarch and served like a gravy over chicken and mashed potatoes or rice.

STIR-FRY CHICKEN   TOP OF STOVE

Quick and easy.

>   3 whole chicken breasts, skinned and boned
>   2 to 3 tablespoons oil
>   1 large onion, sliced
>   1 red or green pepper, cut into thin strips
>   2 cups bean sprouts
>   2 tablespoons soy sauce (or to taste)

Rinse chicken and pat dry. Cut into bite-size pieces. Heat 2 tablespoons oil in wok or large skillet. Add chicken and cook, stirring frequently, until just tender. Remove chicken. Add onion and pepper; cook until just crisp-tender. Add bean sprouts, soy sauce and chicken. Heat through, but do not overcook. You want the vegetables to be crisp. Makes 4 servings.

TIP: If necessary, add the remaining 1 tablespoon oil when cooking the sliced onion and pepper.

CHICKEN AND BROTH   TOP OF STOVE

You can make this recipe go a long way. The chicken can be used for dinner or bones can be removed and the meat can be used for casseroles, salads, soups or sandwiches. The broth can be used in a variety of recipes.

> 1 chicken, cup up
> 1 small onion, quartered and separated
> A few celery tops
> 3 bay leaves
> 1 teaspoon salt
> $^1/_4$ teaspoon pepper

Place all the ingredients in a large pot or Dutch oven. Add 6 cups water to cover. Bring mixture to a boil. Reduce heat; cover and simmer about 1 hour or until chicken is tender.

TIP: For a richer broth, remove chicken and continue to simmer for another hour or so. Strain broth and discard vegetables. To reduce fat content; chill broth and then remove fat solids from top.

SPINACH FILLED BREAST OF CHICKEN   OVEN

Serve with wild rice and hot buttered fresh green beans.

> 4 large chicken breast halves, skinned and boned
> 8 large spinach leaves (remove stems)
> $^1/_2$ cup ham, cut into small narrow strips
> 1 cup (4-ounces) Swiss cheese, grated
> $1^1/_4$ cups whole wheat bread crumbs
> $^1/_3$ cup butter or margarine, melted

Lay chicken on wax paper and gently pound to about $^1/_4$-inch thickness. Place a couple spinach leaves on each chicken breast. Top each with an equal amount of ham and then cheese. Gently fold in the sides and roll, completely covering the filling. (If necessary, use wooden toothpicks to seal.) Dip in melted butter; roll in bread crumbs to coat. Place on baking sheet; brush with additional butter. Bake at 450° for 45 minutes or until cooked through and golden brown. Brush with butter, if chicken appears dry. Makes 4 servings.

CHICKEN CORDON BLEU IN A DISH

TOP OF STOVE
OVEN

An easier and quicker way to prepare Cordon Bleu. This is also a good way to use up that last bit of ham.

> **4 chicken breast halves, skinned and boned**
> **6 tablespoons butter or margarine, divided**
> **3^1/$_2$ cups cooked rice (rice should be hot)**
> **1 cup small cubed cooked ham**
> **1^1/$_2$ cups (6-ounces) grated Swiss cheese**
> **1 teaspoon dried parsley**

Lightly brown chicken in 3 tablespoons of the butter or margarine. Place rice in greased 7x11-inch shallow baking dish. Toss rice with remaining 3 tablespoons butter. Add ham, grated cheese and parsley; mix well. Place chicken on top. Bake at 350° for 40 to 45 minutes or until heated through and chicken is tender. Makes 4 servings.

SOY CHICKEN

TOP OF STOVE
OVEN

Ready to bake in less than ten minutes.

> **1 chicken, cut up**
> **^{1}/$_2$ cup firmly packed light brown sugar**
> **^{1}/$_2$ cup soy sauce**
> **^{1}/$_4$ cup butter or margarine**

Place chicken, skin-side down, in 9x13-inch baking dish. Combine remaining ingredients in small saucepan and place over low heat until butter is melted; stir to mix well. Pour over chicken. Bake at 350° for 30 minutes. Turn and bake 20 to 30 minutes or until done, basting occasionally. Serve some of the sauce with the chicken. Makes 4 servings.

TIP: For appetizers, use the two meaty joints of chicken wings and cook as above. Delicious served hot or at room temperature.

CHICKEN FAJITAS

TOP OF STOVE

When serving both chicken and beef fajitas, the chicken fajitas will be the most popular. I always make more chicken than I think I will need and rarely is there any left over.

> 6 chicken breast halves, skinned and boned
> 3 tablespoons oil
> Dash paprika
> 8-inch flour tortillas, warmed
> Salsa
> Guacamole or sour cream

Cut chicken into bite-size pieces or 1-inch strips. Quickly sauté in heated oil, stirring frequently. Chicken should be tender, but not over-cooked. Sprinkle lightly with a little paprika. Place some of the chicken on each tortilla, top with salsa and guacamole or sour cream. Fold tortilla around filling. Should serve 4 people.

TIP: My favorite way to eat chicken Fajitas is with Onions and Peppers (below). Sometimes I add salsa or sour cream.

ONIONS AND PEPPERS

TOP OF STOVE
BROIL

Serve with Chicken Fajitas.

> 1$^{1}/_{2}$ tablespoons oil
> $^{1}/_{4}$ teaspoon paprika
> $^{1}/_{2}$ red pepper, cut into narrow strips
> $^{1}/_{2}$ green pepper, cut into narrow strips
> 2 onions, thinly sliced, separated into rings
> Salt and pepper to taste

Heat oil in large skillet or wok. Stir in paprika. Add peppers and onion. Cook, stirring frequently, until vegetables are crisp tender. Fill tortillas with chicken and onion-pepper mixture. Fold tortilla around filling; roll up your sleeves and enjoy.

TIP: The servings will depend on how much filling each person uses on a tortilla. In most cases, this recipe will probably serve 4 people.

FAJITA MARINADE

MARINATE

The most popular way to prepare Fajitas is to first marinate the chicken. I don't think this is always necessary. By the time you put eveything else on the Fajita you often lose the flavor of the marinade. But if you want to use a marinade, this is a very quick and easy one.

   $^1/_2$ **cup oil**
   2 tablespoons lemon or lime juice
   2 cloves garlic, minced

Combine all the ingredients; mix well. Add chicken strips and marinate 2 to 3 hours. Drain off as much marinade as possible before cooking. Makes enough marinade for 6 large chicken breast halves.

CHICKEN FRITTATA

TOP OF STOVE
BROIL

   1 to 1$^1/_2$ cups cubed cooked chicken
   $^1/_4$ **cup milk**
   6 eggs
   $^1/_4$ **teaspoon salt**
   2 tablespoons butter or margarine
   $^1/_2$ **cup medium salsa**

Combine milk, eggs and salt; mix well with a fork, but don't beat. Heat butter or margarine in an oven-proof 10-inch skillet. Sprinkle chicken evenly over bottom of skillet. Pour egg mixture over top. Spoon salsa evenly over eggs. Cook over low heat 6 to 8 minutes or until almost set. Broil about 6 inches from heat, 2 to 3 minutes, or until set. Cut into wedges and serve immediately. Makes 4 servings.

SOFT CHICKEN TACOS   OVEN

> For each taco:
> 1 (10-inch) flour tortilla, heated until soft
> Sour cream
> $^1/_2$ cup shredded lettuce
> $^1/_3$ cup cubed cooked chicken (warm)
> Grated Cheddar cheese (about $^1/_3$ cup)
> Salsa

Tortillas can be warmed by wrapping in foil and heating in a 350° oven or place in heated skillet or on hot griddle and heat on both sides just until soft, but not crisp. If tortillas are even the slightest bit crisp, you will have difficulty folding around the filling.

     Quickly spread each tortilla with a small amount of sour cream. Sprinkle lettuce down center. Top with chicken, cheese and salsa. Fold sides and ends over to enclose filling.

TIP: If the tortilla is too full, you will have trouble folding the tortilla around the filling.

SUPER CHICKEN TACO   TOP OF STOVE

An interesting taco. It reminds me of a giant clam shell partially opened.

> For each taco:
> Oil
> 1 (10-inch) flour tortilla
> 1 cup shredded lettuce
> $^1/_2$ to $^3/_4$ cup cubed cooked chicken (warm or cold)
> $^1/_2$ cup chopped tomato
> Sour cream

In large 10-inch skillet, pour oil to a depth of $^1/_2$-inch. Heat to 370°. Add tortilla; cook 15 seconds. Turn; cook about 15 seconds. Remove with tongs and carefully and quickly bend in center to resemble a half open clam shell. Place on paper towels. Place a crumbled piece of foil in opening to hold its shape. Let cool. Place on dinner plate. Add lettuce, top with chicken, then tomato and sour cream. Makes 1 large serving.

VARIATION: To substitute for the tomato and sour cream, use grated Cheddar cheese and salsa.

TACOS IN A BREAD BOWL

TOP OF STOVE
OVEN

So easy children can make them, yet they will draw "ahhhhs" from your guests.

1 pound boneless chicken breast, skinned
1 (1.25-ounce) package taco seasoning mix
1 (10-ounce) can refrigerator Hungry Jack Flaky Biscuits
Shredded lettuce
Chopped tomatoes
Grated Cheddar cheese

Spray a large skillet generously with cooking spray (like Pam or Mazola). Chop chicken in food processor until finely chopped, but not a paste. Add chicken to skillet and cook over medium heat, stirring frequently, until cooked through but not dry. Add seasoning mix and $^3/_4$ cup water; mix well. Cook, over low heat, 8 to 10 minutes or until most of the liquid is absorbed.

Meanwhile, generously grease outside of five 10-ounce custard cups. Separate biscuits. Press 2 biscuits together; roll out to a 5-inch circle on lightly floured surface. Place over outside of inverted custard cups; press evenly over bottom and around sides, pressing almost to edge. Place on baking sheet and bake at 375° for 18 to 20 minutes or until lightly browned. Remove from cups and fill with chicken, layer with lettuce, tomatoes and cheese. If desired, serve with salsa and sour cream. Makes 5 servings.

TIP: If you like a lot of chicken filling, use only 4 of the bread bowls or increase chicken to $1^1/_4$ pounds. Chicken mixture can also be served on a dinner plate or in soft or crisp taco shells. To substitute, add salsa to the cooked chicken and omit the taco seasoning mix. Bread bowls can also be used for serving chili or stew.

CHICKEN TACOS
TOP OF STOVE

Chicken Tacos are becoming almost as popular as ground beef tacos.

> **4 chicken breast halves, skinned and boned**
> **2 tablespoons oil**
> **6 to 8 taco shells**
> **Taco sauce or salsa**
> **Shredded lettuce**
> **Grated Cheddar cheese**

Wash chicken breasts and pat dry. Cut into small bite-size pieces. Toss with oil. Place chicken in large skillet over medium-high heat. Cook until tender, stirring frequently. Remove chicken from skillet and place on paper towels to absorb some of the oil. Place an equal amount of chicken in each taco shell. Top with taco sauce, lettuce and grated cheese. Make 6 to 8 tacos.

CHICKEN WITH SHERRIED SAUCE
TOP OF STOVE

Tender chicken breasts in a creamy sherry flavored sauce.

> **4 to 6 chicken breast halves**
> **Salt and pepper**
> **$1/4$ cup oil**
> **$2/3$ cup dry sherry**
> **4 tablespoons flour**
> **$1^1/4$ cups milk**

Sprinkle chicken with salt and pepper. Brown both sides in hot oil in heavy skillet. Add sherry; bring to a boil. Cover and simmer 30 minutes or until chicken is tender. Remove chicken and keep warm. Bring liquid to a boil. Add flour and quickly stir to blend. Add milk, all at once, stirring constantly until smooth. Cook, until sauce thickens, stirring occasionally. Add additional salt to taste. Boil about 1 minute. Serve sauce with chicken. Makes 4 to 6 servings.

TIP: If sauce is too thick, stir in a little more milk.

CURRIED CHICKEN BAKE

OVEN

Just a touch of curry.

>   **1 chicken, cut up**
>   **$^1/_2$ cup mayonnaise**
>   **2 teaspoons curry powder**
>   **$^1/_2$ teaspoon prepared horseradish**
>   **$^1/_2$ teaspoon soy sauce**
>   **$^1/_2$ teaspoon Dijon mustard**

Place chicken, skin-side down, in greased 9x13-inch baking dish. Combine remaining ingredients; mix well. Brush chicken pieces with sauce. Turn chicken and brush evenly with remaining sauce. Bake at 350° for 60 minutes or until nicely browned. Makes 4 servings.

TIP: Curry is always good with rice. You might want to serve a rice pilaf with peas or white rice cooked with chicken broth.

CHICKEN MORNAY

TOP OF STOVE

Serve over hot buttered toast, noodles or rice.

>   **$1^1/_2$ to 2 cups cubed cooked chicken**
>   **$^1/_4$ cup butter or margarine**
>   **$^1/_4$ cup flour**
>   **2 cups milk**
>   **$^1/_2$ cup (2-ounces) grated Swiss cheese**
>   **Salt and pepper to taste**

Heat butter or margarine in medium saucepan. Stir in flour and cook about a minute. Remove pan from heat; add milk all at one time. Stir until smooth. Return to heat; continue cooking, stirring frequently, until slightly thickened. Add cheese; stir until melted. Season with salt and pepper. Add chicken. Makes 3 to 4 servings.

TIP: If sauce is too thick, gradually stir in additional milk, a little at a time, until desired consistency.

QUICK CHICKEN AND DUMPLINGS

TOP OF STOVE

A quick and easy recipe with a wonderful flavored broth.

> 1 chicken, cut up
> 3 (14$\frac{1}{2}$-ounces) cans Swanson's Chicken Broth
> 1$\frac{1}{2}$ cups flour
> $\frac{1}{2}$ teaspoon baking powder
> $\frac{1}{4}$ cup shortening
> $\frac{1}{2}$ cup milk

Place chicken in large pot. Pour broth over chicken to cover. Simmer, covered, for 45 minutes or until chicken is tender. Meanwhile, combine flour and baking powder. Cut in shortening. Add milk; mix well. Turn out on floured surface and knead lightly 4 to 5 times. Roll out to $\frac{1}{8}$-inch thickness (no thicker). Cut into $\frac{1}{2}$-inch strips about 3 inches long. Drop dumplings into pot; stir lightly. Cover; simmer 20 minutes. Makes 4 to 6 servings.

TIP: Chicken pieces can be served whole with broth and noodles or meat can be removed from bones and returned to pot before adding dumplings.

COMPANY PINEAPPLE CHICKEN

TOP OF STOVE
BROIL

Serve on your most attractive serving dish and garnish with crab apples and parsley.

> 4 chicken breast halves, skinned and boned
> $\frac{3}{4}$ cup flour
> 6 to 8 tablespoons oil
> 4 thin slices boiled ham
> 4 slices canned pineapple
> 4 slices Swiss or Monterey Jack cheese

Place each chicken breast half on wax paper; pound to an even thickness. Dip both sides in flour. Sauté in heated oil over medium high heat (about 3 minutes per side). Place chicken on baking sheet; top each with a slice of ham (fold to fit top of chicken), pineapple and cheese. Place under broiler and broil until cheese is melted and bubbly. Makes 4 servings.

POTATO FLAKE CHICKEN

OVEN

Attractive to serve and has a nice crunch.

4 to 6 chicken breast halves, skinned
1 (5-ounce) can evaporated milk or $^3/_4$ cup milk
$1^1/_2$ teaspoons salt
$^1/_8$ teaspoon pepper
1 to $1^1/_2$ cups instant mashed potato flakes
$^1/_4$ cup butter or margarine, melted

Wash chicken and pat dry. In shallow bowl, combine milk, salt and pepper. Put potato flakes in another bowl. Dip chicken in milk, then in potato flakes, then again in milk, then in potato flakes, turning to coat evenly. Place on greased baking sheet and bake at 350° for $1^1/_2$ hours, basting with melted butter or margarine the last 30 minutes. Chicken should be tender and golden brown. Makes 4 to 6 servings.

CHICKEN STROGANOFF

TOP OF STOVE

If you like beef stroganoff you will have to try this recipe.

4 chicken breast halves, skinned and boned
6 tablespoons butter or margarine, divided
1 cup chopped onion
4 tablespoons flour
$1^3/_4$ cups well seasoned chicken broth
1 cup sour cream

Cut chicken into bite-size chunks or strips. Heat 2 tablespoons of the butter or margarine in large heavy skillet. Add onion; cook until tender but not brown. Remove onion and set aside. Add remaining butter to skillet. Add chicken; cook 4 to 5 minutes or until tender. Sprinkle flour over chicken; stir to mix. Slowly add broth, stirring until smooth. Add onion. Cook until thickened, stirring occasionally. Reduce heat. Add sour cream and heat, but do not let boil. Makes 4 servings.

TIP: Serve over rice or noodles. For added color serve over spinach noodles. If you are not using a well seasoned chicken broth, you may need to add salt and pepper to taste.

CHICKEN SAUSAGE

CHILL
TOP OF STOVE

This recipe may surprise you. Sausage made with chicken is very good.

> **2 pounds chicken breasts, skinned and boned**
> **³/₄ teaspoon freshly ground pepper**
> **³/₄ teaspoon salt**
> **¹/₄ teaspoon cayenne pepper**
> **1 teaspoon dried sage**
> **1 teaspoon dried leaf thyme**

Coarsely chop chicken in a food processor, using about ¹/₄th of the chicken at a time, and an on-off motion. Combine with remaining ingredients; mix well. Chill overnight to blend flavors. When ready to serve, make into patties and cook in a small amount of butter or margarine. Recipe can be halved.

TIP: Spices can be adjusted to your own taste.

KAY'S BAKED ITALIAN CHICKEN

OVEN

A family favorite.

> **1 chicken, cut up**
> **¹/₄ cup butter or margarine, melted**
> **¹/₃ cup Bisquick**
> **¹/₃ cup grated Parmesan cheese**
> **¹/₂ teaspoon garlic powder**
> **1 tablespoon Italian seasoning**

Wash chicken, but do not pat dry. Pour butter into 9x13-inch baking pan. Combine remaining ingredients; blend well. Coat chicken with flour mixture. Place, skin-side down, in pan. Bake 35 minutes. Turn and bake 15 minutes or until done. Makes 4 servings.

CHICKEN ITALIAN

Preparation time has been kept to a minimum with this quick and easy recipe.

>   4 chicken leg-thigh pieces
>   2 tablespoons butter or margarine, melted
>   1 (14^1/$_2$-ounce) can Italian style stewed tomatoes, with juice
> ^{1}/$_2$ teaspoon oregano
>   2 tablespoons cornstarch

Place chicken, skin-side up, in 9x13-inch baking dish. Pour melted butter or margarine over top. Bake at 425° for 45 minutes, basting a couple of times with drippings. Meanwhile, pour stewed tomatoes in small saucepan. Cut larger pieces of tomatoes into smaller pieces. Add oregano. Add about 2 tablespoons of juice from tomatoes to cornstarch; mix until smooth. Add to tomatoes; cook over low heat until thickened. This takes just a couple of minutes. Pour over chicken. Bake 15 minutes. Makes 4 servings.

CHICKEN TORTELLINI

Depending on how much you like tortellini, this is more of a side dish than the main course.

>   1 large clove garlic, minced
>   1 tablespoon olive oil
>   2 (14.5 ounce) cans whole Italian style tomatoes, cut up
>   1 tablespoon sugar
>   8 or 9 ounce package chicken tortellini

In medium saucepan, cook garlic in olive oil, but do not brown. Add tomatoes with juice. Stir in sugar. Bring to a boil; reduce heat and simmer 45 minutes or until thickened. Meanwhile, cook tortellini according to package directions. Drain and rinse. Serve tomato sauce over tortellini. Makes 4 servings.

CHICKEN PARMESANNA   TOP OF STOVE

4 chicken breast halves, boned and skinned
$2/3$ cup seasoned Italian bread crumbs
$1/3$ cup grated Parmesan cheese
$1/2$ cup butter or margarine, melted, divided
$1/2$ cup marinara or spaghetti sauce
4 slices Mozzarella cheese

Place each chicken breast half between wax paper and flatten slightly. Mix bread crumbs and Parmesan cheese together. Dip chicken in $1/4$ cup of the melted butter or margarine, then into bread crumb mixture. Heat remaining butter or margarine in large skillet. Add chicken and brown on both sides. Top each chicken half with some of the sauce and then a slice of the cheese. Cover and cook 5 minutes or until cheese is melted and chicken is cooked through. Makes 4 servings.

CHICKEN PARMESAN BAKE   OVEN

A scrumptious blend of flavors.

4 to 6 chicken breast halves
$1/4$ cup freshly grated Parmesan cheese
1 cup seasoned Italian bread crumbs
$1/4$ cup butter

Combine Parmesan cheese and bread crumbs. Roll chicken in crumb mixture to coat. Place chicken, skin-side up, on greased baking sheet. Bake at 350° for 60 minutes or until golden brown, brushing occasionally with melted butter. Makes 4 servings.

TIP: Serve with hot Fetticcine Romano, page 162, and green peas. Add a tossed salad and roll and you have an easy, but delicious dinner.

TORTILLA CHICKEN PIZZAS

Delicious chicken pizza using flour tortillas for the crust. This is an easy recipe to increase or decrease.

1 red and 1 green bell pepper
1 large onion, sliced and separated into rings
6 (8-inch) flour tortillas
1 cup pizza sauce (approximately)
3 cups (12-ounces) grated Mozzarella cheese
2 cups cooked chicken breast, cut into small narrow strips

Cut peppers into narrow strips. Place in large skillet along with onion. Add 2 tablespoons water. Cover; cook over medium heat until vegetables are just crisp tender. Drain. Place flour tortillas on baking sheets. Bake at 400° for 5 to 6 minutes. Do not eliminate this step or your pizzas will be soggy. Remove tortillas from oven and turn over. Spread each tortilla with 2$\frac{1}{2}$ to 3 tablespoons of pizza sauce. Sprinkle each with equal amounts of Mozzarella, then chicken. Top with some of the onion mixture. Increase temperature to 450°. Bake pizzas 10 minutes or until cheese is melted. Makes 6 pizzas.

TIP: If desired, substitute butter or margarine for the water

CHICKEN PIZZA

An especially filling way to use leftover chicken.

1$\frac{1}{4}$ cups cubed cooked chicken
1 can refrigerator pizza dough
$\frac{3}{4}$ cup pizza sauce (more or less)
16 ounces Mozzarella cheese, grated
1 medium onion, sliced and separated into rings
$\frac{1}{2}$ cup each of red and green pepper, sliced into strips

Press pizza dough onto greased 14-inch pizza pan or 11x15-inch jelly roll pan. Spread layer of pizza sauce over dough. Distribute chicken evenly over sauce. Sprinkle with cheese. Top with onion rings, then top with pepper strips. Bake at 500° for 12 to 14 minutes or until crust is golden brown; do not let the cheese brown. Makes 4 to 6 servings.

TIP: A pizza pan with tiny holes or a pizza stone will produce a crisper crust on the bottom.

CHICKEN LASAGNA

TOP OF STOVE
OVEN

A nice change from ground beef.

2 cups cubed cooked chicken
8 lasagna noodles, cooked
1¹/₂ cups dry curd ricotta cheese
3 cups chunky style spaghetti sauce
3 cups (12-ounce) grated Mozzarella cheese
¹/₃ cup freshly grated Parmesan cheese

Place 4 of the noodles in bottom of greased 7x11-inch shallow baking dish. Combine chicken and spaghetti sauce. Pour half the mixture over noodles. Spread ricotta evenly over top. Sprinkle with half the grated Mozzarella. Repeat layers. Sprinkle with grated Parmesan. Bake at 350° for 40 to 45 minutes or until heated through. Let stand 10 minutes before serving. Makes 4 to 6 servings.

CHICKEN WITH TOMATOES

TOP OF STOVE

An easy dinner meal.

6 chicken legs or thighs
2 tablespoons oil
1 small onion, sliced, separated into rings
1 (14.5-ounce) can stewed tomatoes, with juice
1 (6-ounce) jar marinated artichoke hearts, drained
Salt and pepper to taste

Brown chicken in heated oil in large skillet. Remove chicken and set aside. Add onion to skillet and cook about 2 minutes (add a bit more oil, if necessary). Add tomatoes, artichokes and salt and pepper to taste. Return chicken to skillet; spoon some of the sauce over the top. Cover and simmer for 45 minutes. Makes 3 to 4 servings.

CHICKEN-SAUSAGE KABOBS

Delicious served with rice pilaf, Chinese pea pods and hot buttered rolls.

> **4 chicken breast halves, skinned and boned**
> **Salt and pepper**
> **12 (1-inch) pieces link-type Italian sausage**
> **12 large whole mushrooms**
> **$1/4$ cup butter or margarine, melted**

Cut chicken in 1 to $1^1/2$-inch chunks, sprinkle with salt and pepper. Simmer sausage pieces in a little water 5 to 6 minutes or until partially cooked. Arrange chicken, sausage and mushrooms on skewers. Grill 6 to 7 minutes on each side, basting occasionally with butter or margarine, until done. Makes 4 servings.

TIP: Your favorite marinade or sauce can be substituted for the butter or margarine.

CHICKEN-SEAFOOD KABOBS

> **3 chicken breast halves, skinned and boned**
> **8 mushrooms**
> **1 red pepper, cut in large squares**
> **8 jumbo shrimp, peeled and de-veined**
> **4 green onions, cut in 2 inch lengths**
> **Vegetable oil**

Cut chicken into large bite-size pieces. Alternate food on skewers, using chicken, mushroom, red pepper, shrimp, and small bunches of green onion strips. Begin and end with chicken. Place kabobs on oiled grill. Brush lightly with oil. Cook, turning several times, until cooked through, basting frequently with oil. Makes 4 servings.

CHICKEN HAWAIIAN

OVEN

A family and company favorite.

> **4 large chicken breast halves, skinned and boned**
> **4 pineapple spears**
> **4 tablespoons shredded coconut**
> **1 teaspoon salt**
> **$^1/_2$ cup unseasoned dry bread crumbs**
> **$^1/_2$ cup butter or margarine, melted**

Place each chicken breast half between wax paper; gently pound to about $^1/_4$-inch thickness. Place a pineapple spear toward one end of chicken. Sprinkle with 1 tablespoon coconut. Fold edges over and roll to enclose filling. Secure with toothpicks. Combine salt and bread crumbs. Dip chicken in melted butter; coat with bread crumbs. Place on greased baking sheet. Bake at 350° for 40 to 50 minutes or until golden. If chicken appears dry, brush with butter. Makes 4 servings.

TIP: Serve with rice pilaf, sautéed bananas and tossed salad. If desired serve Rich Cream Sauce, page 52, or Mornay Sauce, page 53, over chicken.

SESAME CHICKEN

MARINATE
TOP OF STOVE, OVEN

This may seem like a lot of brown sugar, and it is, but only a tiny bit of the sauce clings to the chicken.

> **1 chicken, cut up (do not remove skin)**
> **2 cups firmly packed light brown sugar**
> **1 cup soy sauce**
> **2 cloves garlic, minced**
> **2 to 3 drops sesame oil**

Place chicken in 9x13-inch baking dish. Combine remaining ingredients in medium saucepan; mix well. Cook over medium heat until sugar is dissolved. Pour over chicken, turning to coat. Cover; refrigerate several hours or overnight, basting occasionally with the sauce.

When ready to bake, pour off marinade and reserve. Place chicken, skin side up, in greased baking dish and bake at 375° for 45 minutes, basting frequently with some of the sauce. Makes 4 servings.

TIP: Lining the baking dish with foil will make cleaning a lot easier.

DELICIOUS APRICOT CHICKEN

OVEN

An all time favorite.

    1 chicken, cut up
    1 cup apricot jam or preserves
    1 (8-ounce) bottle Russian salad dressing
    2 teaspoons curry powder
    1 package dry onion soup mix

Place chicken, skin-side up, in greased 9x13-inch baking dish. Combine remaining ingredients. Spoon over top of chicken. Bake at 350° for 30 minutes. Baste chicken. Continue cooking 30 minutes, basting occasionally. Makes 4 servings.

GLAZED CHICKEN

OVEN

A different combination of ingredients for a familiar recipe.

    1 chicken, cut up
    1 cup apricot preserves
    $^{1}/_{2}$ cup bottled Russian dressing
    $^{1}/_{4}$ cup mayonnaise
    1 package dry onion soup mix

Place chicken, skin-side up, in greased 9x13-inch baking dish. Combine remaining ingredients and pour over chicken. Bake at 350° for 60 minutes or until well glazed and tender, brushing frequently with the sauce. Makes 4 servings.

APRICOT-PINEAPPLE CHICKEN

MARINATE
OVEN

    6 chicken breast halves
    1 (16-ounce) bottle Italian dressing
    $1^{1}/_{4}$ cups apricot-pineapple preserves

Place chicken in shallow dish. Pour dressing over top. Cover; marinate at least a couple of hours or overnight. Remove chicken; place, skin-side up, in a buttered 9x13-inch baking dish. Combine $1^{1}/_{4}$ cups of the dressing with the preserves. Pour over chicken. Cover and bake at 325° for 60 minutes. Uncover and bake 30 to 40 minutes or until chicken is tender and nicely glazed. Makes 6 servings.

DILLY CHICKEN

TOP OF STOVE
OVEN

If you like the flavor of dill, you will enjoy this recipe.

> **4 to 6 chicken breast halves, skinned**
> **$^3/_4$ cup sour cream**
> **1 cup chicken broth**
> **2 tablespoons flour**
> **1 teaspoon dried dill weed**
> **1 teaspoon sugar**

Place chicken in buttered 9x13-inch baking dish. Combine remaining ingredients in small saucepan. Bring to a boil and cook, stirring occasionally, until thickened. Pour over chicken, spreading to coat. Bake at 350° for 60 minutes. Increase oven to 375° and cook 30 minutes. Makes 4 to 6 servings.

TORTELLINI BAKE

TOP OF STOVE
OVEN

> **8 to 9 ounces chicken tortellini, cooked**
> **2 cups (8-ounces) grated Cheddar cheese**
> **1 (15.5 ounce) jar spaghetti sauce**
> **2 tablespoons grated Parmesan cheese**

Place cooked tortellini in greased 9x9-inch baking dish. Sprinkle grated Cheddar cheese over top. Pour spaghetti sauce over cheese and sprinkle with Parmesan. Bake at 350° for 20 minutes or until heated through. Makes 6 servings.

Cook's Tip

Calories can be reduced by removing chicken skin and all fat before cooking.

GARLIC CHICKEN

A mild-flavored garlic chicken that is so tender it just falls off the bone.

> **1 chicken, cut up**
> **Salt and pepper**
> **$^1/_2$ cup flour**
> **3 tablespoons oil**
> **40 cloves garlic, unpeeled**
> **$^1/_2$ teaspoon Italian seasoning**

Sprinkle chicken with salt and pepper. Coat with flour. Brown chicken in heated oil in a large Dutch oven. Remove paper-like covering from garlic cloves, but do not peel. Add garlic to pan stirring to coat with some of the oil. Sprinkle with seasoning. Add $^1/_2$ cup water. Cover and bake at 350° for 1$^1/_2$ hours. Makes 4 servings.

TIP: If you have nice large garlic cloves, use only 30, but if you are using the smaller ones most supermarkets carry, use 40.

VARIATION: For a nice flavor change, add a little bit of lemon juice and oregano or thyme and omit the Italian seasoning.

EASY CREAM CHICKEN

Lots of flavor for such a simple recipe.

> **1 chicken, cut up**
> **Salt and pepper**
> **2 tablespoons butter or margarine**
> **$^1/_2$ cup chopped onion**
> **3 tablespoons water**
> **1 cup whipping cream**

Sprinkle chicken with salt and pepper. Melt butter or margarine in heavy skillet. Add chicken and brown lightly on both sides. Add onion and cook 2 to 3 minutes. Add water. Cover and cook over low heat for 30 minutes or until chicken is tender. Add cream; stir to blend. Cook, uncovered, 5 to 10 minutes or until cream has thickened slightly. Serve sauce over chicken. Makes 4 servings.

EASY BAKED CHICKEN   OVEN

Treat yourself to a quick and easy meal.

1 chicken, quartered
$^1/_4$ cup butter or margarine
Paprika
Salt and pepper

Place chicken, skin-side up, in 7x11-inch baking dish. Dot with small pieces butter. Sprinkle with paprika, salt and pepper. Bake at 400° for 60 minutes or until golden brown, basting frequently with the drippings (add more butter, if necessary). Serve with rice, green beans and French bread. Makes 4 servings.

TIP: If larger servings are desired, use one half chicken per person.

HONEY-MUSTARD CHICKEN   OVEN

A nicely glazed curry-flavored chicken.

4 to 6 chicken breast halves, skinned
$^1/_2$ cup honey
$^1/_2$ cup butter or margarine, melted
$^1/_4$ cup prepared mustard
1 teaspoon curry powder

Place chicken, skin-side up, in buttered 9x13-inch baking dish. Combine remaining ingredients and spoon over chicken. Bake at 350° for 60 minutes, basting frequently with the sauce. Makes 4 to 6 servings.

Cook's Tip

Poultry is very perishable and should be refrigerated at all times. It should be stored in its original wrapping in the coldest part of the refrigerator. Poultry should be used as soon as possible and no longer than 1 to 2 days after purchasing.

EASY HAWAIIAN CHICKEN

TOP OF STOVE
OVEN

    1 chicken, cut up or 4 chicken breast halves
    $1/2$ cup flour
    $1/4$ cup butter or margarine
    $1/2$ cup soy sauce
    3 tablespoons sugar
    1 (20-ounce) can pineapple chunks, save juice

Coat chicken with flour. Heat butter or margarine in skillet and brown chicken. Place chicken with butter in greased 9x13-inch baking dish. Combine soy sauce, sugar and juice from pineapple; pour over chicken. Cover; bake at 350° for 60 minutes. Uncover; add pineapple and bake 20 minutes. Makes 4 servings.

GRILLED ROSEMARY CHICKEN

MARINATE
GRILL

Because of the small amount of oil in this recipe, you will have less flare-up when grilling.

    1 chicken, cut up
    $1/4$ cup oil
    $1^1/2$ cups orange juice
    1 teaspoon dried rosemary
    Salt and pepper

Wash chicken and pat dry. Place in bowl or plastic container. Combine remaining ingredients and pour over chicken. Marinate 2 to 3 hours or overnight. When ready to cook, remove chicken from marinade and place on heated grill. Cook slowly, turning often, until chicken is tender, about 40 minutes. To prevent chicken from drying out, brush frequently with marinade. Makes 4 servings.

ROSEMARY

ITALIAN GRILLED CHICKEN

MARINATE
GRILL

This is a perfect busy day recipe.

1 chicken, cut-up
Italian dressing (your favorite brand)

Marinate chicken in dressing several hours or overnight. Remove from marinade and place, skin-side down, on grill. Baste frequently with a small amount of dressing (watch carefully for flare-ups). Cook 30 minutes, turn and slowly cook until tender, basting frequently. Makes 4 servings.

VARIATION: To make ahead, bake chicken in 350° oven, about 45 minutes or until tender, basting frequently with the dressing. When ready to serve, reheat on grill, basting with desired barbecue sauce.

JARLSBERG STUFFED CHICKEN BREASTS

OVEN

An easy stuffed chicken recipe.

4 large chicken breast halves, skinned and boned
4 fingers Jarlsberg cheese, about $2^1/_3$x$^1/_2$-inches
Basil (optional)
Salt and pepper
$^1/_3$ cup milk
$^1/_2$ cup dry unseasoned bread crumbs

Place each chicken breast half between wax paper. Pound evenly to about $^1/_4$-inch thickness. Place one finger of cheese about an inch from one of the short ends. Sprinkle with salt and pepper and just a few sprinkles of basil. Starting with short end, roll up, tucking in sides and completely enclosing the cheese. Secure with a couple wooden tooth-picks. Dip chicken in milk. Coat with bread crumbs. Place in shallow baking pan and bake at 350° for 40 minutes or until cooked through. Makes 4 servings.

TIP: While baking, if the chicken appears dry, baste with a little melted butter or margarine.

ITALIANO CHICKEN

OVEN

Your kitchen will smell "sooooo" good.

excellent! Tim loved it!!!

- 4 chicken breast halves, skinned and boned
- $1/2$ cup grated Parmesan cheese
- $1/2$ teaspoon dried oregano
- 1 teaspoon garlic salt
- $1/4$ teaspoon ground black pepper
- $1/4$ cup butter or margarine, melted

Wash chicken breasts and pat dry. Combine Parmesan cheese, oregano, garlic salt and pepper. Dip both sides of chicken in the melted butter; coat with cheese mixture. Place on shallow baking pan. Pour remaining butter or margarine over top. Bake at 375° for 30 to 40 minutes or until chicken is tender and golden brown. If chicken is a little dry, brush with some of the butter. Makes 4 servings.

TIP: Serve with hot buttered noodles, Italian green beans and marinated tomato slices.

TROPICAL CHICKEN

OVEN
TOP OF STOVE

Leftovers are even good cold.

- 6 chicken breast halves, skinned and boned
- $1/4$ cup butter or margarine, melted
- $1/3$ cup maple flavored syrup
- 2 tablespoons honey
- 1 (8-ounce) can crushed pineapple, with juice
- 1 tablespoon cornstarch

Place chicken in shallow 2-quart baking dish. Pour melted butter or margarine over chicken. Bake at 350° for 30 minutes. Meanwhile, in small saucepan, combine remaining ingredients and mix well. Bring to a boil, reduce heat and simmer 8 to 10 minutes or until thickened. Spoon over chicken; increase temperature to 375° and bake 10 minutes longer or until nicely glazed. Makes 4 to 6 servings.

LEMON BASIL CHICKEN   TOP OF STOVE

If you like lemon you will enjoy this quick and easy recipe.

> **4 chicken breast halves, skinned and boned**
> **$^1/_2$ cup flour**
> **4 tablespoons butter or margarine**
> **1 small lemon, with peel**
> **1 cup chicken broth**
> **1 teaspoon dried basil**

Place each chicken breast half between wax paper and flatten slightly. Roll in flour to coat. Melt butter or margarine in large skillet. Brown chicken on both sides, about 3 minutes each side. Add 3 tablespoons lemon juice from the lemon and grated peel from the rind. Add broth and basil. Cover and simmer 10 minutes. Remove chicken and keep warm. Bring liquid to a boil and cook until reduced to about $^1/_2$ cup. Spoon sauce over chicken and serve. Makes 4 servings.

LEMON CHICKEN   TOP OF STOVE
                                               OVEN

A definite lemon flavor.

> **4 chicken breast halves, skinned and boned**
> **Salt and pepper**
> **$^3/_4$ cup chicken broth**
> **$^1/_4$ cup white wine**
> **2 large lemons**
> **3 teaspoons flour**

Place each chicken breast half on wax paper and pound to an even thickness. Sprinkle with salt and pepper. Spray a large skillet with Pam. Over medium heat, brown chicken lightly on both sides. (Add more Pam, if necessary.) Remove chicken. To the pan, add the broth and wine; bring to a boil. Meanwhile, squeeze $^1/_4$ cup juice from one of the lemons. Combine juice and flour until smooth. Add to skillet; cook until thickened, stirring frequently.

    Place chicken in 8x8-inch baking pan. Pour sauce over top. Slice remaining lemon and distribute over chicken. Bake at 375° for 20 minutes. Serve chicken topped with sauce and lemon slices. Makes 4 servings.

LEMON PEPPER CHICKEN   TOP OF STOVE

This makes a quick spur-of-the-moment recipe with a nice lemon-pepper flavor.

>   **4 to 6 chicken breast halves, skinned and boned**
>   **1 cup flour**
>   **1 tablespoon seasoning salt**
>   **2 tablespoons lemon pepper**
>   **1/4 cup lemon juice**
>   **1/2 cup butter or margarine**

Wash chicken and pat dry. Place each chicken piece on wax paper and gently pound to about 1/4-inch. Combine flour, salt and lemon pepper. Dip chicken in lemon juice; coat with flour mixture. Heat butter in a large heavy skillet. Add chicken and cook over medium heat until golden brown and chicken is cooked through, about 3 to 4 minutes each side. Drain on paper towels to remove excess butter. Makes 4 to 6 servings.

TIP: This is also a nice way to prepare chicken strips. Just follow the above recipe, but cut chicken breasts into long narrow strips.

LOW CALORIE CHICKEN CHILI   TOP OF STOVE

>   **1 pound boneless chicken breast halves, skinned**
>   **1 cup chopped onion**
>   **2 teaspoons chili powder**
>   **2 (16-ounce) cans tomatoes, with liquid**
>   **1 (16-ounce) can kidney beans, drained**
>   **Salt and pepper to taste**

Wash and dry chicken. Cut into small pieces and process in blender or food processor until coarsely chopped. Cook in large skillet that has been sprayed heavily with Pam. Add chopped onion and cook along with the chicken. Stir in chili powder, tomatoes (cut-up), beans, salt and pepper. Cook, over low heat, about 60 minutes to blend flavors. Makes 4 servings.

POPOVER CHICKEN

I am frequently asked for good salt-free recipes. This one is very good, but if you are accustomed to salt, you may wish to add a teaspoon to the batter.

1 chicken, cut up
$^1/_3$ cup, plus $1^1/_2$ cups flour
7 tablespoons butter or margarine, divided
$1^1/_2$ teaspoons baking powder
$1^1/_2$ cups milk
4 eggs, slightly beaten

Coat chicken with the $^1/_3$ cup flour. Heat 4 tablespoons of the butter in a large skillet. Brown chicken on all sides. Remove chicken and set aside. Combine remaining $1^1/_2$ cups flour and baking powder. Combine milk, eggs and remaining 3 tablespoons butter, melted. Add to flour mixture, beating until smooth. Pour into buttered 9x13-inch baking dish. Arrange chicken on top, skin-side up. Bake at 350° for 60 minutes or until golden. Serve right away as batter tends to fall as it sits. Makes 4 servings.

MARINARA SAUCE WITH CHICKEN

A flavorful mixture of ingredients.

2 tablespoons butter or margarine
$^1/_2$ cup sliced green pepper
1 cup sliced onion, separated into rings
1 cup sliced fresh mushrooms
2 ($15^1/_2$ -ounce) jars marinara sauce
$1^1/_2$ to 2 cups cubed cooked chicken

Heat butter in large skillet; sauté green pepper and onion 3 to 4 minutes. Add mushrooms and cook 1 to 2 minutes. Add marinara sauce; cook over low heat about 20 minutes, stirring occasionally. Add chicken and cook 10 minutes. Makes 4 servings.

TIP: Serve over hot wide noodles, angel pasta or tortellini.

LEMON ROASTED CHICKEN
OVEN

A subtle lemon flavor.

> 1 (4 to 6 pound) roasting chicken
> $^3/_4$ cup butter or margarine, softened
> 1 large lemon (use for lemon peel, juice and lemon slices)
> Salt and pepper to taste

Wash chicken and pat dry. Place on rack in roasting pan. Combine butter or margarine with grated peel from lemon. Cut lemon in half. Squeeze 2 tablespoons juice from one of the halves. Add to butter mixture. Add salt and pepper. Starting at the neck of the chicken, loosen the skin by carefully slipping your fingers between the skin and the meat; work down to the legs, being careful not to tear the skin. With a small spatula or your fingers, spread half the butter mixture under the skin. Pat skin to make a smooth layer.

Slice remaining lemon half and place in chicken cavity. Truss chicken (if desired). Rub with some of the remaining butter mixture. Roast at 375° for 1 to 1$^1/_2$ hours or until done, brushing frequently with remaining butter mixture. Makes 4 servings.

STUFFED ROAST CHICKEN
OVEN

A roast chicken should serve four, but the average roast chicken in most supermarkets is so small it will feed only two or three hearty appetites.

> 1 (4 to 6 pound) roasting chicken
> $^1/_2$ cup melted butter or margarine, divided
> 3 cups seasoned bread stuffing mix
> $^2/_3$ cup water
> $^1/_4$ teaspoon poultry seasoning
> $^1/_2$ teaspoon paprika

Wash chicken and pat dry. Place on rack in roasting pan. Combine $^1/_3$ cup of the butter with stuffing mix, water and poultry seasoning. Stuff chicken lightly. Bake at 375° for 30 minutes. Combine remaining butter and paprika. Brush some of the mixture over chicken. Continue baking 30 to 45 minutes or until tests done, basting occasionally with remaining butter mixture. Makes 4 servings.

OVEN CHICKEN AND GRAVY

TOP OF STOVE
OVEN

The secret to making good gravy is to use a wire whisk.

> 1 chicken, cut up
> Salt and pepper
> $^3/_4$ cup flour, divided
> 4 tablespoons butter or margarine
> $2^1/_2$ cups milk
> $^1/_3$ cup dry sherry

Sprinkle chicken with salt and pepper. Roll in $^1/_2$ cup of the flour to coat. Brown in heated butter or margarine. Remove from skillet and place in 9x13-inch baking dish. Add remaining $^1/_4$ cup flour to drippings in skillet. Stir until smooth and starts to bubble. Add milk; quickly stir to blend. Continue to cook until thickened, stirring frequently. Stir in sherry and cook 3 to 4 minutes. Add salt and pepper to taste. Pour over chicken. Cover with foil. Bake at 350° for 45 minutes or until chicken is tender. Stir sauce to make a smooth gravy and serve over chicken. Makes 4 servings.

TIP: If desired, remove skin from chicken; it will not get crisp during baking.

MUSTARD BAKED CHICKEN

OVEN

A lot of flavor for a small amount of work.

> 1 chicken, cut up
> $^1/_2$ cup flour
> $^1/_2$ cup butter or margarine, melted
> $^3/_4$ teaspoon dry mustard
> Seasoning salt

Coat chicken pieces with flour. Combine melted butter and dry mustard in shallow flat bowl. Dip chicken in mixture to coat. Place, skinside up, in greased 9x13-inch pan. Sprinkle with seasoning salt. Bake at 400° for 50 to 60 minutes, basting frequently with the drippings. Makes 4 servings.

MAYO CHICKEN   OVEN

Good family fare.

1 chicken, cut up
$1/2$ cup mayonnaise
2 teaspoons Dijon mustard
2 teaspoons honey
$1^1/4$ cups fine cracker crumbs

Wash chicken and pat dry. Combine mayonnaise, mustard and honey. Brush chicken pieces with mixture. Roll in crackers crumbs to coat. Place chicken, skin-side up, on baking sheet. Bake at 350° for 60 minutes or until golden brown. Makes 4 servings.

NO OIL TERIYAKI CHICKEN   MARINATE
                                                         GRILLL

A very tasty low-calorie teriyaki sauce is used in this recipe.

1 chicken, cut up, skin removed
$2/3$ cup lite soy sauce
$1/4$ cup white wine
2 tablespoons sugar
$1/2$ teaspoon ground ginger (or use fresh ginger slices)
1 garlic clove, minced

Wash chicken and pat dry. Combine remaining ingredients and pour over chicken. Marinate 2 to 3 hours or overnight. Remove chicken from marinade and place on oiled grill. Cook until tender, turning and basting frequently. Cooking time will take 45 to 60 minutes. Makes 4 servings.

GARLIC

ONE POT CHICKEN DINNER   OVEN

This recipe takes less than 10 minutes to prepare and it can bake in the oven while you do something else.

> 1 chicken, cut up or 4 chicken breast halves
> 4 to 6 medium potatoes, peeled and quartered
> Garlic salt
> Paprika
> Oregano
> $1/4$ cup butter or margarine

Place potatoes in bottom of large casserole or Dutch oven. Place chicken on top, skin-side up. Sprinkle chicken lightly with a little garlic salt, paprika and oregano. Cut butter or margarine into small pieces and distribute over top. Cover and bake at 450° for 60 minutes. Makes 4 servings.

TIP: If desired, carrots, cut into thirds, can be added along with the potatoes.

ONION PEPPER CHICKEN   TOP OF STOVE

An economical recipe served as a stir-fry or as a filling for warmed flour tortillas.

> 2 chicken breast halves, skinned and boned
> 2 tablespoons oil, divided
> 3 small onions, sliced and separated into rings
> $1^1/2$ green peppers, cut into strips
> $1/2$ red pepper, cut into strips
> Salt and pepper to taste

Cut chicken into bite-size chunks or strips. Toss with 1 tablespoon of the oil. Place in large skillet or wok. Cook over high heat, stirring frequently, until cooked through. Remove from skillet. Add onion and remaining oil; cook until slightly softened, stirring frequently. Add green and red pepper strips; salt and pepper to taste. Continue cooking until vegetables are cooked, but still slightly crisp. Add chicken. Makes 4 servings.

OVEN-BAKED PECAN CHICKEN

A wonderful recipe with a delightful crunch and flavor.

4 to 6 chicken breast halves
1 cup biscuit mix
$^1/_2$ teaspoon poultry seasoning or paprika
$^1/_2$ cup very finely chopped pecans
$^1/_2$ cup half-and-half
$^1/_2$ cup melted butter or margarine

Combine biscuit mix, poultry seasoning and pecans; mix well. Dip chicken in half-and-half, then in crumb mixture, coating both sides. Place, skin-side up, in a 7x11-inch baking dish. Pour melted butter over top. Bake at 375° for 50 minutes or until golden brown, basting occasionally with the butter. Makes 4 to 6 servings.

TIP: Milk or canned evaporated milk can be substituted for the half-and-half.

ORIENTAL CHICKEN WITH PINEAPPLE   TOP OF STOVE

For a quick and easy dinner, this recipe can be prepared in about 20 minutes.

2 whole chicken breasts, skinned and boned
$^1/_4$ cup butter or margarine
1 (20-ounce) can pineapple chunks (save juice)
1 small green pepper, cut into narrow strips
2 tablespoons soy sauce
4 teaspoons cornstarch

Cut chicken into bite-size pieces. Heat butter in heavy skillet and quickly sauté the chicken pieces until tender. Add one cup of the pineapple chunks and the green pepper. Combine $^3/_4$ cup of the pineapple juice, soy sauce and cornstarch; mix until smooth. Add to chicken mixture and cook, stirring constantly, until thickened. Cook over low heat until green pepper is just tender. (If mixture thickens too much, stir in a little pineapple juice.) Makes 4 servings.

TIP: Chicken is delicious served over rice. Start the rice at the same time you start the chicken. Also, if you use a lite soy sauce, you may wish to add a little salt to the recipe.

PINEAPPLE-CHUTNEY CHICKEN
OVEN

Something a little different.

> 4 to 6 chicken breast halves, skinned
> 1 (8-ounce) can crushed pineapple, do not drain
> $^{1}/_{2}$ cup Major Grey's chutney
> $^{1}/_{4}$ cup prepared mustard
> $^{1}/_{2}$ cup chopped walnuts or pecans

Place chicken, skin-side up, in greased 7x11-inch baking dish. Combine remaining ingredients and pour over top. Bake at 350° for 1 hour and 15 minutes. (No need to turn or baste.) Makes 4 to 6 servings.

CHICKEN WITH SPANISH RICE
TOP OF STOVE

Lots of flavor with just a few ingredients.

> 1 chicken, cut up
> 2 tablespoons oil
> 1 (14$^{1}/_{2}$-ounce) can stewed tomatoes
> 1 medium onion, sliced, separated into rings
> 1 cup uncooked long-grain rice
> 1$^{1}/_{2}$ to 2 teaspoons salt

Brown chicken in hot oil in deep 10-inch skillet. Pour juice from tomatoes into a large measuring container. Add water to measure 2$^{1}/_{2}$ cups. Pour into skillet; add remaining ingredients. (Make sure all the rice is covered with liquid.) Bring to a boil. Reduce heat; cover and cook over low heat 30 to 40 minutes or until liquid is absorbed and rice is tender. Makes 4 servings.

Cook's Tip

Ovens can vary in the amount of time it takes to bake certain foods. Make a note along side each recipe if the baking time varies from yours.

ROAST CORNISH HENS OVEN

Especially good for a company meal.

4 Cornish hens
$1/4$ cup butter or margarine, melted
Salt and pepper
$1/3$ cup honey
$1/3$ cup apricot nectar

Wash hens and pat dry. Place on rack in roasting pan. Brush with melted butter or margarine. Sprinkle lightly with salt and pepper. Bake at 425° for 30 minutes. Combine honey and apricot nectar. Brush hens with some of the sauce. Continue baking 30 minutes or until tender and nicely glazed, brushing frequently with the sauce. Makes 4 servings.

CORNISH HENS WITH HONEY GLAZE OVEN

Cornish Hens are always nice for small families and/or small appetites. They are also very attractive served whole for special dinner parties.

2 Cornish hens
$1/2$ cup honey
1 tablespoon soy sauce
1 teaspoon grated orange peel (or narrow strips)
2 tablespoons orange juice

Place Cornish hens on rack in roasting pan. Combine remaining ingredients; mix thoroughly. Brush a small amount on chicken. Bake at 425° for 30 minutes, brushing once with more glaze. Bake an additional 30 minutes or until tender, brushing frequently with the glaze. Makes 2 large or 4 small servings.

CHICKEN BROCCOLI CASSEROLE WITH RICE

TOP OF STOVE
OVEN

1 (20-ounce) package frozen broccoli, chopped or spears
5 cups cooked long-grain rice
2¹/₂ cups cubed cooked chicken
2 cans cream of chicken soup
1 cup mayonnaise
2 cups (8-ounces) grated Mozzarella cheese, divided

Place frozen broccoli in a colander and run under hot water. Drain thoroughly. Spread on bottom of greased 9x13-inch baking dish. Top with the cooked rice. Combine chicken, soup, mayonnaise and 1 cup of the grated cheese. Pour over rice. Sprinkle with remaining 1 cup cheese. (The dish will be quite full.) Bake at 350° for 30 to 35 minutes or until golden. Watch carefully the last few minutes. Makes 6 to 8 servings.

TIP: Omit chicken and you have a delicious vegetable-rice dish.

SWISS CHICKEN CASSEROLE

TOP OF STOVE
OVEN

A great way to use leftover chicken.

2 to 3 cups cubed cooked chicken
1 cup uncooked long-grain rice, cooked
¹/₄ cup butter or margarine
1¹/₄ cups milk
3 eggs, beaten
2 cups (8-ounces) Swiss cheese, grated

Place chicken in large mixing bowl. Combine hot rice with the butter; stir until butter is melted. Add to chicken along with the remaining ingredients. Pour into buttered 7x11-inch baking dish. Bake at 350° for 45 minutes or until set. Makes 6 servings.

VARIATION: Use half chicken and half ham.

SOUR CREAM NOODLE CASSEROLE

TOP OF STOVE
OVEN

A great way to use up that last 2 cups of leftover chicken.

> 3 cups cooked egg noodles, drained
> 2 cups cubed cooked chicken
> 1 cup creamed cottage cheese
> 1^1/$_2$ cups sour cream
> 1 (2^1/$_4$-ounce) can sliced ripe olives, drained
> 6 tablespoons grated Parmesan cheese, divided

Cook noodles according to directions on package. Meanwhile, combine remaining ingredients in large mixing bowl, using 3 tablespoons of the Parmesan cheese. Add cooked noodles. Pour into greased 7x11-inch baking dish. Sprinkle with remaining Parmesan cheese. Bake at 350° for 40 minutes. Makes 4 to 6 servings.

CHICKEN DIVINE CASSEROLE

TOP OF STOVE
OVEN

A tasty combination of flavors.

> 4 cooked chicken breast halves
> 2 cups broccoli spears, cooked
> 1 (8-ounce) package cream cheese, softened
> 1 cup milk
> ^{3}/$_4$ teaspoon garlic salt
> ^{3}/$_4$ cup Parmesan cheese

Cut chicken, lengthwise, into about ^{1}/$_4$-inch slices. Place in buttered 9x9-inch shallow baking dish. Top with broccoli spears (cut into smaller pieces). In mixer bowl, whip cream cheese; slowly add milk. Pour into medium saucepan; add garlic salt and Parmesan cheese. Cook, over low heat, until thickened. Pour over broccoli. Bake at 350° for 35 to 40 minutes. Makes 4 servings.

TIP: If you have leftover chicken or turkey, you can substitute for the chicken breast.

CHICKEN WITH MUSHROOMS & ARTICHOKES   TOP OF STOVE
OVEN

If you like artichokes you will enjoy this recipe.

     4 to 6 chicken breast halves, skinned and boned
     4 tablespoons butter or margarine
     6 ounces (2 cups) sliced fresh mushrooms
     1 (14-ounce) jar marinated artichoke hearts, drained
     2 tablespoons flour
     1$\frac{1}{2}$ cups chicken broth

Lightly brown chicken in heated butter in large skillet. Place in 9x9-inch baking dish. Add mushrooms to skillet (adding 1 tablespoon butter, if necessary). Sauté until lightly browned. Remove mushrooms with a slotted spoon and sprinkle over chicken. Place artichoke hearts around chicken. Add flour to remaining butter in skillet; stir to blend. Add broth and cook until slightly thickened, 3 to 4 minutes. Pour over chicken. Cover; bake at 350° for 45 minutes. Makes 4 to 6 servings.

TIP: Depending on how deep your baking dish is, you may not use all of the sauce.

OVEN CHICKEN PILAF   OVEN

This is sure to make everyone happy.

     4 chicken breast halves
     Salt and pepper
     2 tablespoons melted butter or margarine
     2 cups hot chicken broth
     1 cup uncooked long-grain rice
     $\frac{1}{3}$ cup slivered almonds, toasted

Place chicken, skin-side up, in greased 9x13-inch baking dish. Sprinkle with salt and pepper. Brush with the melted butter. Bake at 350° for 30 minutes. Add $\frac{1}{2}$ cup water to baking dish and bake 10 minutes. Remove from oven. Pour hot broth into baking dish. Add rice to liquid, distributing evenly. Sprinkle almonds over top. Cover tightly with foil and bake 30 minutes. Remove foil and bake about 10 minutes or until liquid is absorbed and chicken is golden. Makes 4 servings.

Perfect Fried Chicken

SOUTHERN FRIED CHICKEN   TOP OF STOVE

There are several ways to prepare Southern Fried Chicken, depending on who you talk to, but many Southerners agree that the only way to cook the chicken is to pan-fry it in lard. With our awareness of cholesterol, many of us may cringe at even the thought of using lard, but the flavor (and tradition) is there.

> **1 chicken, cut up**
> **$1/2$ cup flour**
> **1 teaspoon salt**
> **$1/4$ teaspoon pepper**
> **1 cup lard**

Wash chicken and pat dry. Combine flour, salt and pepper. Roll chicken in flour to coat. Heat lard in deep frying pan. Add chicken and cook, turning frequently, until browned and cooked through, about 20 to 25 minutes. Remove and drain on paper towels. Makes 4 servings.

BUTTERMILK FRIED CHICKEN   TOP OF STOVE

If you like crunchy fried chicken you will love this recipe.

> **1 chicken, cut up**
> **Salt and pepper**
> **1 cup flour**
> **1 cup buttermilk**
> **Oil**

Wash chicken and pat dry. Sprinkle with salt and pepper. Coat on all sides with flour. Dip in buttermilk and again in flour. Heat about $1^{1}/4$-inches oil in a deep heavy skillet. Cook chicken in hot oil, about 20 to 30 minutes, turning once. Drain on paper towels. Makes 4 servings.

CORNMEAL FRIED CHICKEN

TOP OF STOVE

A nice crisp coating.

> 1 chicken, cut up
> ³/₄ cup yellow cornmeal
> ³/₄ cup flour
> Salt and pepper
> ¹/₂ cup milk
> Oil

Combine cornmeal, flour, salt and pepper. Dip chicken in milk and coat with flour mixture. Heat about 2-inches oil in a large heavy skillet. Add chicken and cook until golden; turn and brown other side. Cook until tender, about 20 minutes total cooking time. Drain on paper towels. Makes 4 servings.

COUNTRY FRIED CHICKEN

TOP OF STOVE

> 1 chicken, cut up
> 1 ¹/₂ cups flour
> 2 teaspoons salt
> 1 ¹/₄ teaspoon ground black pepper
> ¹/₂ cup milk
> Oil

Combine flour, salt and pepper. Coat chicken with flour mixture. Dip in milk, then back in flour to cover. Heat ¹/₂-inch oil in large heavy skillet. Add chicken and brown both sides. Continue cooking, turning frequently, about 20 to 25 minutes or until chicken is cooked through. Don't cook chicken too fast or coating will get much too dark. Makes 4 servings.

TIP: This makes a crunchy coating. For less crunch, omit the first coating of flour.

EASY BAKED FRIED CHICKEN   OVEN

An easy way to fry chicken without using flour.

1 chicken, cut up
Salt and pepper
Paprika
6 tablespoons butter or margarine

Sprinkle both sides of chicken with salt, pepper and paprika. Place chicken, skin-side down, in greased 9x13-inch baking pan. Dot with butter. Cover with foil. Bake in 400° oven for 30 minutes. Remove foil. Increase temperature to 425° and bake 30 minutes. Turn chicken; bake 15 to 20 minutes or until nicely browned, basting frequently with pan drippings. Makes 4 servings.

FRIED CHICKEN STRIPS   TOP OF STOVE

Nice finger food.

4 large chicken breast halves, boned and skinned
$^1/_2$ cup flour
1 teaspoon salt
$^1/_4$ teaspoon pepper
$^1/_2$ cup buttermilk (yogurt or sour cream)
Oil

Cut chicken into 1-inch wide strips. Combine flour, salt and pepper. Dip chicken in buttermilk, then coat with flour. Heat about $^1/_2$-inch of oil in large skillet. Fry chicken strips until golden and cooked through (do not overcook or they will be tough). Makes 4 servings.

TIP: Serve Cream Gravy, page 54, over rice or mashed potatoes and top with chicken strips. Add a salad and Sally Lunn Muffins, page 144, for a complete meal.

ITALIAN FRIED CHICKEN   TOP OF STOVE

Just the right blend of spices

> **4 chicken breast halves, skinned**
> **1 cup flour**
> **1 (0.7 ounce) package Italian salad dressing mix**
> **$^1/_3$ cup milk or half-and-half**
> **Oil**

Combine flour and salad dressing mix until blended. Dip chicken in milk and coat thoroughly with the flour mixture. In deep large skillet, pour oil to a depth of 1 inch. Heat oil; add chicken and brown over medium heat. Continue cooking, turning several times until chicken is done, about 20 minutes. Makes 4 servings.

TIP: To bake in the oven: Place, skin-side up, on baking sheet. Brush with a little melted butter. Bake at 350° for 60 minutes or until tender and golden brown.

OVEN FRIED CHICKEN   MARINATE
                                              OVEN

If you are short on time, you don't have to marinate the chicken.

> **1 chicken, cut up**
> **2 cups buttermilk**
> **$^1/_4$ teaspoon ground pepper**
> **$^3/_4$ cup flour**
> **$^3/_4$ cup freshly grated Parmesan cheese**
> **$^1/_4$ cup butter or margarine, melted**

Marinate chicken in buttermilk for at least 2 hours or more. Combine pepper, flour and Parmesan cheese; mix thoroughly. Remove chicken from buttermilk; dip in flour mixture, coating all sides. Place in greased shallow baking pan, skin-side up. Drizzle melted butter or margarine over chicken. Bake at 400° for 60 minutes or until golden brown. Makes 4 servings.

TIP: If you omit marinating, decrease buttermilk to 1 cup. If desired, the skin can be removed and you will still have a beautiful golden crust on the chicken.

OVEN-FRIED CHICKEN WITH HERBS   OVEN

Nice and crisp.

1 chicken, cut up
$^1/_3$ cup melted butter or margarine
$^3/_4$ cup finely crushed Rice Chex cereal
1 teaspoon salt
1 teaspoon paprika
1 teaspoon fine herbs

Wash chicken and pat dry. Dip in melted butter or margarine. Combine remaining ingredients; mix well. Roll chicken in crumbs to coat. Place chicken, skin-side down, on greased baking sheet. Bake at 375° for 30 minutes. Turn chicken; bake 30 minutes or until golden. Makes 4 servings.

Cook's Tip

An attractive way to serve Fried Chicken is in a bread bowl:

1 large round loaf unsliced French, or sourdough bread
Melted butter or margarine
Basil or oregano

Cut top off bread. Remove most of the bread, leaving about a 1-inch shell. Generously butter inside of the bowl. Sprinkle lightly with basil or oregano. Bake at 375° for 10 to 12 minutes or until bread is lightly browned and crisp. Place on serving plate or basket; fill with fried chicken. After the chicken is served, the bread bowl can be eaten. Holds 6 to 8 pieces of chicken, depending on the size of the bread.

QUICK AND EASY FRIED CHICKEN   TOP OF STOVE

Some fried chicken recipes vary so little from other recipes, yet that small difference becomes a family favorite. This is a recipe handed down among southern cooks.

1 chicken, cut up
Salt and pepper
³/₄ cup flour
Oil

Wash chicken, but do not dry. Sprinkle with salt and pepper. Place flour in paper bag. Drop in a few pieces of chicken at a time and shake to coat. Heat about 2-inches oil in large deep and black cast-iron skillet or chicken fryer. Place chicken in hot oil, skin-side down. Cover and cook 10 minutes. Uncover and cook 5 minutes or until golden. Turn and cook, uncovered, 10 minutes or until golden and chicken is cooked through. Makes 4 servings.

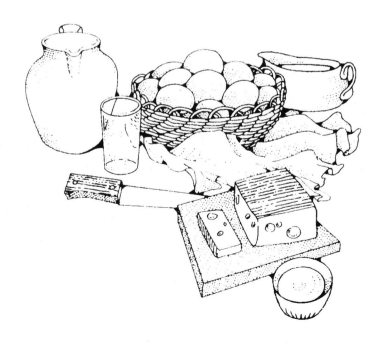

Cooking
with Soup

BAKED SOUR CREAM CHICKEN

TOP OF STOVE
OVEN

4 large chicken breast halves, skinned
4 slices bacon
1 cup sour cream
1 can cream of mushroom soup
1 cup fresh sliced mushrooms
3 tablespoons orange or pineapple juice

Wash chicken and pat dry. Partially pre-cook bacon. It should be limp not crisp. Wrap a slice of bacon around each chicken breast. Place in greased 9x13-inch baking dish. Combine remaining ingredients; pour over chicken. Bake at 350° for 1¹/₂ hours. Makes 4 servings.

MUSHROOM CHICKEN BAKE

OVEN

1 chicken, cut up
¹/₄ cup butter or margarine, melted
1 can cream of mushroom soup
1 teaspoon dried parsley

Place chicken, skin-side down, in 9x13-inch baking dish. Pour butter or margarine over top. Bake at 375° for 20 minutes. Turn chicken; bake 20 minutes. Stir soup. Spoon evenly over chicken. Sprinkle with parsley. Bake 20 minutes. Makes 4 servings.

GOLDEN MUSHROOM CHICKEN

OVEN

1 chicken, cut up
1 medium onion, thinly sliced and separated into rings
1 green pepper, thinly sliced
2 cans Golden Mushroom soup
1¹/₂ soup cans water
2 (4.5-ounce) packages Chicken Flavored Rice with seasonings

Distribute onion and green pepper in greased 9x13-inch baking dish. Combine soup with water, mixing until smooth. Stir in rice; pour over vegetables. Place chicken, skin-side up, on top. Cover with foil and bake at 350° for 60 minutes. Uncover and bake 30 to 40 minutes or until rice is tender and liquid is absorbed. Makes 4 servings.

TIP: If chicken isn't browning, brush with a little melted butter or use some of the liquid from the pan.

CHICKEN AND WILD RICE BAKE   OVEN

Once you put this casserole in the oven you will have some time to relax before getting the rest of the dinner ready.

>   6 chicken breast halves
>   2 cans cream of chicken soup
>   1 cup long grain & wild rice, uncooked
>   1 (5-ounce) can sliced water chestnuts, drained
>   1 package dry onion-mushroom soup mix
>   2 tablespoons melted butter or margarine

Wash chicken and pat dry. In mixing bowl, combine soup with 2 tablespoons water; mix until smooth. Stir in rice, water chestnuts and dry soup mix. Pour into greased 9x13-inch baking dish. Arrange chicken on top, skin-side up. Cover with foil and bake at 325° for 2 hours. Remove foil, brush chicken with melted butter. Increase heat to 350° and bake 15 to 20 minutes or until chicken is browned and liquid is absorbed. Makes 4 to 6 servings.

TIP: If you want more mushrooms, add a 4-ounce can sliced mushrooms (with liquid) and omit the 2 tablespoons water. If the chicken is omited, the rice makes a delicious side dish.

CHICKEN CHINESE CASSEROLE   OVEN

A simple but tasty casserole.

>   3 cups cubed cooked chicken
>   1 (5-ounce) can sliced water chestnuts, halved
>   3³/₄ cups Chow Mein noodles, divided
>   1 cup mayonnaise
>   1 can cream of mushroom soup
>   2 cans cream of chicken soup

Place chicken, water chestnuts and 3 cups of the Chow Mein noodles in large mixing bowl. (Save remaining noodles for top.) Combine remaining ingredients; mix until smooth. Add to chicken mixture. Pour into greased 2¹/₂-quart casserole. Bake at 350° for 50 minutes. Sprinkle remaining Chow Mein noodles over top. Bake 10 minutes or until casserole is heated through. Makes 6 servings.

GREEN BEAN-CHICKEN CASSEROLE

TOP OF STOVE
OVEN

An excellent potluck casserole that will feed several people.

    1 (6-ounce) package Uncle Ben's Long Grain &
       Wild Rice (original recipe)
    3 cups cooked cubed chicken
    1 can cream of celery soup
    2 (16-ounce) cans French style green beans, drained
    1 cup mayonnaise
    1 (5-ounce) can sliced water chestnuts

Cook rice according to directions on package. Meanwhile, in large mixing bowl, combine remaining ingredients. Stir in rice; mix to blend. Pour into a buttered 2$^1/_2$ or 3-quart casserole. Bake at 350° for 60 minutes or until heated through. Makes 8 to 10 servings.

TIP: If baking in a shallow casserole, check after 45 minutes.

CHICKEN-MACARONI CASSEROLE

TOP OF STOVE
OVEN

We can never have too many good casserole recipes. This one is great for pot-lucks as well as everyday family meals.

    3 cups cubed cooked chicken
    3 cups cooked cork-screw shaped noodles
    2 cups (8-ounces) grated Swiss cheese
    1 can cream of chicken soup
    1 cup milk
    $^1/_8$ teaspoon freshly ground pepper

Place chicken, noodles and cheese in greased 2-quart casserole. Combine soup, milk and pepper; mix well. Add to chicken mixture. Bake at 400° for 30 to 40 minutes or until heated through. Makes 6 servings.

TIP: Very good reheated.

CHICKEN SAUSAGE LOAF   OVEN

This may be an unusual meat loaf to many of you, but it is very good.

1 pound uncooked chicken breast, skinned and boned
1 pound bulk sausage
3 eggs
1 can cream of chicken soup
$1^3/_4$ cups rolled oatmeal
$^1/_2$ teaspoon salt

Grind chicken or finely chop in a food processor. Combine with remaining ingredients. (This is sometimes easier to do with your hands.) Ingredients should be well mixed. Pour into greased 9x5-inch loaf pan. Bake at 350° for 60 minutes. Remove from pan; cover with foil and let stand 10 to 15 minutes before slicing. Makes 8 servings.

TIP: Also makes good sandwiches or serve sliced between hot buttered biscuits. Cooking with ground chicken is relatively new for me. The first time I made this recipe I almost threw it away, it looked so awful in its raw state. But the finished product is very good and a recipe you will want to make often.

CHICKEN WITH MUSHROOM SAUCE   TOP OF STOVE

An easy top of the stove recipe that makes a delicious gravy.

4 to 6 chicken breast halves
$^1/_4$ cup butter or margarine
$1^1/_2$ cups sliced fresh mushrooms
2 garlic cloves, minced
1 can cream of mushroom soup
$^2/_3$ cup half-and-half

Brown chicken in heated butter in large skillet. Remove chicken. (If butter is too dark, discard and add 3 tablespoons new butter.) Brown mushrooms and garlic. Stir in soup; mix well. Stir in half-and-half. Add chicken, skin-side up. Cover; cook over low heat 40 minutes. Serve sauce over the chicken or with the chicken. Makes 4 to 6 servings.

TIP: When browning the chicken, do not cook too long or it will be tough.

CHICKEN WITH ALMONDS
OVEN

For a large crowd this is delicious and so easy to prepare.

2 chickens, cut up
$^1/_2$ cup slivered almonds
1 can cream of chicken soup
1 can cream of celery soup
1 can cream of mushroom soup
$^1/_4$ cup vermouth

Place chicken, skin-side up, in large greased shallow roasting pan. Sprinkle a little more than half the almonds over chicken. Combine remaining ingredients and pour over chicken. Sprinkle with remaining almonds. Bake at 350° for 2 hours. Makes 8 servings.

COMPANY CHICKEN AND RICE
OVEN

This is my favorite chicken recipe to use when serving a lot of people. If you want to serve buffet style, bake in your most attractive large casserole dish or roasting pan.

12 chicken breast halves
$1^1/_2$ cups uncooked long-grain rice
1 can cream of celery soup
1 can cream of mushroom soup
1 can cream of chicken soup
$^1/_2$ cup melted butter

Place rice in bottom of a large buttered roasting pan that is at least 2 inches deep. Combine soups in mixing bowl; gradually stir in $1^1/_2$ soup cans water; mix well. Pour over rice. Dip chicken pieces in butter; place, skin-side up, on rice mixture. Bake, uncovered, at 250° for $2^1/_2$ hours or at 350° for $1^1/_2$ hours or until liquid is absorbed, rice is tender and chicken has browned. Makes 12 servings.

VARIATION: Add 1 (4-ounce) can sliced mushrooms and/or $^1/_2$ cup slivered almonds. Substitute white wine for some of the water.

CORNMEAL BISCUIT TOPPED CASSEROLE   OVEN

It is sometimes amazing what you can do with just six ingredients. Here you have chicken, biscuits and gravy, all in one dish.

> **1 chicken, cut up, (skinned, if desired)**
> **2 cans cream of chicken soup**
> **$^1/_2$ cup plus 3 tablespoons milk**
> **$^1/_2$ teaspoon ground ginger**
> **1 cup Bisquick**
> **$^1/_4$ cup yellow cornmeal**

Place chicken pieces in a buttered deep 3-quart casserole. Combine $1^1/_2$ cans of the soup, the $^1/_2$ cup milk and ginger. Pour over chicken. Cover and bake at 350° for 60 minutes. Increase oven to 450°. Combine the remaining $^1/_2$ can soup, the 3 tablespoons milk, Bisquick and cornmeal; stir just until moistened. Remove casserole; drop about 8 mounds of dough over top of chicken. Bake, uncovered, 15 to 20 minutes or until biscuits are golden and cooked through. Makes 4 servings.

CURRIED CHICKEN AND RICE   TOP OF STOVE
                                                OVEN

A wonderful casserole for boating, camping or just a busy day.

> **4 chicken breast halves, skinned and boned**
> **3 tablespoons butter or margarine, divided**
> **1 cup finely chopped onion**
> **3 cups cooked long-grain rice**
> **2 cans cream of chicken soup**
> **1 teaspoon curry powder**

Cut chicken into bite-size pieces. In a large skillet, sauté chicken in two tablespoons of the butter. Cook just until cooked through; do not overcook. Remove chicken. Add remaining one tablespoon butter or margarine and cook onion until tender. Combine onion and chicken with remaining ingredients. Pour into ungreased 2-quart casserole. Bake at 375° for 30 minutes or until heated through. Makes 6 servings.

TIP: This is also a good recipe for that last $1^1/_2$ to 2 cups of left over chicken or turkey you have sitting in the refrigerator. Just cut it up into small cubes and add to the remaining ingredients.

GOLDEN SOUR CREAM CHICKEN   OVEN

Serve this oven baked chicken with rice or noodles.

4 chicken breast halves, skinned
3 tablespoons butter or margarine
1 can cream of chicken soup
¹/₂ cup sour cream
Dried parsley
2 tablespoons sliced almonds

Place chicken, skin-side down, in 7x11-inch baking dish. Dot with butter. Bake at 375° for 20 minutes. Turn chicken, bake 20 minutes. Combine soup and sour cream; spoon over chicken. Sprinkle lightly with parsley and almonds. Bake 20 minutes or until tender. Makes 4 servings.

MEXICAN CHICKEN CASSEROLE   OVEN

A favorite quick and easy casserole.

16 taco shells
2 cups cubed cooked chicken
2 cans cream of chicken soup
1 (10-ounce) can tomatoes with green chilies, undrained
1 cup finely chopped onion
2 cups (8-ounces) grated Cheddar cheese

Crumble taco shells and place in greased 9x13-inch baking dish. Distribute chicken evenly over top. Combine soup and tomatoes with chilies, cutting tomatoes into smaller pieces. Add onion to soup mixture. Pour evenly over chicken. Sprinkle with grated cheese. Bake at 350° for 60 minutes or until liquid is absorbed. Makes 6 servings.

TIP: Most supermarkets carry the Ro-Tel brand of canned tomatoes with chilies.

MUSHROOM CHICKEN SUPREME   OVEN

A can of soup can help save the day.

> 1 chicken, cut up
> 1 can cream of mushroom soup
> 1 (4-ounce) can sliced mushrooms, drained
> 2 tablespoons chopped pimiento
> 1 cup sour cream
> ¹/₂ cup sherry or white wine

Place chicken, skin-side up, in buttered 9x13-inch baking dish. Combine remaining ingredients and spoon over top. Bake at 375° for 60 minutes or until chicken is tender. Makes 4 servings.

BAKED CHICKEN IN MUSHROOM SAUCE   OVEN

> 1 chicken, cut up
> Salt and pepper
> 1 can cream of mushroom soup
> 1 cup grated Cheddar cheese
> 1 teaspoon whole sage, crushed
> 4 green onions, sliced (use both green and white part)

Place chicken, skin-side up, in greased 9x13-inch baking dish. Sprinkle with salt and pepper. Combine remaining ingredients; pour over chicken. Bake at 400° for 60 minutes or until tender, basting occasionally. Makes 4 servings.

SPECIAL CREAM CHICKEN

TOP OF STOVE
OVEN

The sauce makes a wonderful gravy to serve over rice.

1 chicken, cut up
1/2 cup flour
Salt and pepper
1/2 teaspoon paprika (optional)
1/4 cup oil
1 can cream of chicken soup

Wash chicken and pat dry. Combine flour, salt, pepper and paprika. Coat chicken with flour mixture. Heat oil in heavy skillet and lightly brown chicken. Place chicken, skin-side up, in greased 7x11-inch baking dish. Stir chicken soup and pour over top. Bake at 350° for 60 minutes or until chicken is tender. Makes 4 servings.

TENDER BAKED MUSHROOM CHICKEN

OVEN

A moist flavorful chicken.

1 chicken, cut up
1 1/2 cups chopped onion
1 teaspoon mixed herbs
1 tablespoon Worcestershire sauce
1 can cream of mushroom soup

Spread onion in bottom of greased 9x13-inch baking dish. Place chicken, skin-side up, on top. Sprinkle evenly with herbs. Combine Worcestershire sauce and soup; spoon over chicken. Cover tightly and bake at 350° for 30 minutes. Uncover, raise heat to 375° and bake about 45 minutes or until lightly browned. Serve sauce over chicken. Makes 4 servings.

CURRIED CHICKEN BREASTS

A light curry flavor.

> 4 chicken breast halves
> $^1/_4$ cup oil
> 1 teaspoon curry powder (or to taste)
> 1 can cream of chicken soup
> 1 cup sour cream
> $^1/_4$ cup sliced almonds

Lightly brown chicken in hot oil. Place in greased 7x11-inch baking dish. Mix curry with soup; pour over chicken. Bake at 350° for 45 minutes. Spoon sour cream over chicken; sprinkle with almonds. Return to oven; bake 10 to 15 minutes or until bubbly. Makes 4 servings.

TIP: If desired, stir pan drippings together and serve over chicken.

Cook's Tip

Maximum Suggested Freezing Times
0° F (-20°C)

Uncooked chicken	12 months
Cooked chicken	1 month
Cooked chicken covered with a broth or gravy	6 months
Cooked chicken casseroles	6 months
Fried chicken	4 months

Company

Menus

Linda's Phyllo Chicken and Broccoli

Wild Rice with Pecans
Julienned Carrots
Romaine Salad
Jiffy Dinner Rolls
Pineapple Jubilee

Grocery List:

6 chicken breast halves
2 large bunches romaine lettuce
$2^1/_2$ cups broccoli flowerettes
2 pounds carrots
$^1/_3$ cup wild rice
1 cup long-grain rice
1 package dry yeast
$2^2/_3$ cups chicken broth
1 (9-ounce) box white or yellow
  Jiffy cake mix
1 (20-ounce) can pineapple
  chunks
$^1/_2$ cup orange marmalade
1 package Phyllo
$^1/_2$ gallon vanilla ice cream
$^1/_2$ cup pecans
4 tablespoons Grand Marnier liqueur
2 cups sour cream
1 cup grated Parmesan cheese

On Hand:

Salt and pepper
1 garlic clove
2 tablespoons cider vinegar
2 tablespoons light corn syrup
5 tablespoons light brown sugar
3 cups flour
6 tablespoons olive oil
$1^1/_2$ cups plus 1 tablespoon
  butter

Short Cut:

Can prepare chicken day ahead
Buy dinner rolls
Make pineapple sauce ahead

Serves 6 to 8

LINDA'S PHYLLO CHICKEN AND BROCCOLI

TOP OF STOVE
OVEN

This is one of my daughters favorite company recipes. She likes to prepare it the day before and bake just before serving. Very elegant and even good cold.

6 chicken breast halves, cooked, cut into small pieces
2^1/$_2$ cups broccoli flowerettes
2 cups sour cream
10 sheets Phyllo
1 cup butter, melted
1 cup freshly grated Parmesan cheese

Steam the broccoli until it turns bright green and is not quite crisp tender (don't overcook). Rinse with cold water to stop the cooking process. Cut the flowerettes into small pieces and set aside. Combine the chicken and sour cream and set aside .

Lay out one sheet of phyllo (keep remaining phyllo covered with wax paper and a slightly damp towel to prevent drying out). Brush with melted butter. Top with second sheet of phyllo and brush with butter. Repeat until you have 5 sheets. Spread phyllo with half the chicken mixture, leaving a 2-inch border all the way around. Sprinkle with half the broccoli and half the Parmesan cheese. Fold the 2-inch border over, covering outer edge of filling. Brush with butter. Starting with short end, roll up jelly-roll style. Place, seam-side down, on baking sheet. Brush with butter. Repeat with second half of ingredients.Bake at 375° for 20 to 25 minutes or until golden (may take longer if rolls have been refrigerated). Slice each roll into 4 to 6 slices. Makes 6 to 8 servings.

TIP: Hearty appetites will want 2 slices. Rolls can be made day ahead and refrigerated.

JULIENNED CARROTS

TOP OF STOVE

A favorite carrot recipe.

2 pounds carrots, peeled and cut julienne style
^{1}/$_2$ cup butter, melted
3 tablespoons light brown sugar
Salt and pepper to taste

Place carrots in large saucepan. Pour butter over top. Add brown sugar. Cook over medium heat, until carrots are crisp tender, about 15 minutes. Season with salt and pepper to taste. Makes 6 to 8 servings.

WILD RICE WITH PECANS   TOP OF STOVE

A perfect rice dish for a special company dinner.

$^1/_3$ **cup wild rice**
2$^2/_3$ cups chicken broth
1 cup long-grain rice
$^1/_2$ **cup coarsely chopped pecans**
1 tablespoon butter or margarine

Wash wild rice well under cold running water for about a minute (this is easier to do in a strainer). In a medium saucepan, combine the wild rice and chicken broth. Bring to a boil. Reduce heat, cover and simmer 20 minutes. Add white rice and bring to a boil. Reduce heat, cover and simmer 20 minutes or until liquid is absorbed and rice is tender. Meanwhile, lightly toast pecans in heated butter. Gently stir pecans into the rice mixture. Makes 6 to 8 servings.

ROMAINE SALAD   CHILL

There are times when you want a rather simple but tasty salad. This one will go with almost any meal.

2 large bunches romaine lettuce
6 tablespoons olive oil
2 tablespoons apple cider vinegar
1 large garlic clove, peeled, thinly sliced
$^1/_2$ **teaspoon salt**
$^1/_8$ **teaspoon freshly ground pepper**

Wash romaine; tear into bite-size pieces and chill until ready to serve. Combine remaining ingredients; let stand at room temperature 1 to 2 hours. When ready to serve, remove garlic from dressing. Place romaine in salad bowl and toss with just enough dressing to coat. Makes 6 to 8 servings.

TIP: For an extra special dinner, garnish with a tomato wedge and sprinkle lightly with freshly grated Parmesan cheese.

JIFFY DINNER ROLLS

OVEN

My mother told me about this recipe. The cake mix is quite different, but the rolls are delicious and very easy to prepare.

1 (9-ounce) box white or yellow Jiffy cake mix
1 package dry yeast
$1/2$ teaspoon salt
$1^1/4$ cups hot tap water
$2^1/2$ to 3 cups flour

In large mixing bowl, combine cake mix, yeast and salt. Stir in water and flour to make a soft dough. (Dough will be quite sticky.) Cover and let rise until double, 1 to $1^1/2$ hours. Stir down dough and spoon onto a well-floured surface. Gently turn dough a couple times to lightly coat with flour. Shape into desired size rolls and place on greased baking sheets. Or shape into balls and place in greased muffin tins. Cover and let rise until double, about 1 hour. Bake at 400° for 10 to 15 minutes or until golden. Makes 15 to 18 rolls depending on size desired.

PINEAPPLE JUBILEE

TOP OF STOVE

Perfect for a special dinner party.

1 (20-ounce) can pineapple chunks, drained
$1/2$ cup orange marmalade
2 tablespoons light corn syrup
2 tablespoons light brown sugar
4 tablespoons Grand Marnier liqueur
Vanilla ice cream, frozen hard

Combine first four ingredients in chafing dish or large skillet; mix well. Cook, over low heat, until heated through. Heat liqueur in small saucepan until just warm (do not overheat). Carefully flame liqueur and immediately pour over pineapple mixture. Scoop ice cream into champagne glasses or deep dessert dishes. Serve pineapple sauce over ice cream. Makes 6 to 8 servings.

TIP: This is a fun recipe to flame at the table, but watch carefully, you don't want to burn anything.

VARIATION: Sprinkle with toasted sliced almonds or shredded coconut if desired.

Chicken Elegant

Company Rice Casserole
Snow Peas with Cashews
Orange-Onion Romaine Salad
Refrigerator Dinner Rolls
Ice Cream with Amaretto

Grocery List:

4 whole boned chicken breasts
5 cups assorted salad greens
$^1/_2$ pound snow peas
1 small red onion
1 medium onion
2 oranges
1 lemon
$^3/_4$ cup frozen peas
$^1/_2$ gallon vanilla ice cream
$3^1/_2$ cups chicken broth
1 (7-ounce) box Wild Pecan Rice
  (Konriko brand)
$^1/_2$ cup cashews
2 tablespoons sliced almonds
2 packages dry yeast
4 tablespoons Amaretto liqueur
$^1/_2$ pint whipping cream
1 cup half-and-half

On Hand:

Salt and pepper
1 garlic clove
1 tablespoon dried parsley
$^1/_2$ cup sugar
5 cups flour
$2^1/_2$ tablespoons olive oil
$^1/_2$ cup shortening
1 cup butter
3 eggs

Short Cut:

Serve hot buttered frozen peas
Buy dinner rolls

Serves 4

CHICKEN ELEGANT

4 boned whole chicken breasts
$1/3$ cup plus 3 tablespoons butter
1 cup seasoned chicken broth
$1/4$ cup flour
1 cup half-and-half
Salt and pepper

Chicken breasts should be left whole with bones removed (do not remove skin). Heat the $1/3$ cup butter in heavy skillet. Tuck chicken breast ends under, shaping into a nice round. Brown bottom side first, turn and brown top side. Place in shallow baking dish. Add chicken broth. Cover with foil and bake at 375° for 60 minutes or until tender. Remove chicken and keep warm (reserve broth). Melt 3 tablespoons butter in small saucepan; stir in flour until blended. Remove from heat; stir in reserved broth and half-and-half. Cook, stirring frequently, until mixture boils and thickens. Season with salt and pepper. Place chicken on serving plate; pour sauce over top. Makes 4 servings.

COMPANY RICE CASSEROLE

This is a delightful rice casserole with a slightly nutty taste. It can be served with almost any type of main dish.

3 tablespoons butter
1 cup finely chopped onion
1 (7-ounce) box Wild Pecan Rice (Konriko brand)
1 teaspoon salt
1 tablespoon dried parsley
$2^{1}/2$ cups chicken broth

Heat butter in medium size skillet. Add onion; cook about one minute. Add rice; cook 3 to 4 minutes or until onion is soft, stirring occasionally. Pour into a greased $2^{1}/4$ or $2^{1}/2$-quart deep casserole. Stir in remaining ingredients. Cover and bake at 375° for 50 to 60 minutes or until liquid is absorbed and rice is tender. Gently stir to distribute the parsley that floats to the top. Makes 6 servings.

SNOW PEAS AND CASHEWS

TOP OF STOVE

$^1/_2$ **pound snow peas, ends trimmed**
$^3/_4$ **cup frozen peas**
2 tablespoons butter
1 garlic clove, minced
$^1/_2$ **cup cashews, split**
Salt and pepper

Add snow peas to large skillet or wok and cover with water. Cook until just crisp tender. Remove snow peas and set aside. Add frozen peas to water; cook until thawed, but not soft. Remove peas and discard water. Add butter to pan and heat. Add garlic, cashews, salt and pepper; simmer 1 to 2 minutes. Add the peas and gently toss to mix. Makes 4 servings.

TIP: If you have 2 green onions in the refrigerator you don't know what to do with, cut them into 1-inch pieces and add to the butter mixture.

ORANGE-ONION ROMAINE SALAD

One of my favorite quick salads with a light orange-flavored dressing.

5 cups assorted salad greens
4 thin slices red onion, separated into rings
1$^1/_2$ seedless oranges
2$^1/_2$ tablespoons olive oil
1$^1/_2$ teaspoons lemon juice
Salt and pepper to taste

Place greens in salad bowl; add onion. Peel oranges; cut into thin slices. Take a couple of the slices and squeeze to get about 1$^1/_2$ teaspoons of juice. Cut remaining slices into quarters and add to salad. Combine orange juice with remaining ingredients; mix well. Add dressing to salad, adding just enough to lightly coat leaves; toss gently. Serve immediately. Makes 4 servings.

REFRIGERATOR DINNER ROLLS   OVEN

You will find this recipe convenient when you have a busy week, but still want delicious homemade rolls for a special dinner. Dough can be made ahead and refrigerated overnight.

> **2 packages dry yeast**
> **3 eggs, beaten lightly**
> **$1/2$ cup shortening**
> **$1/2$ cup sugar**
> **$1^1/2$ teaspoons salt**
> **$4^1/2$ cups flour**

Combine yeast and 1 teaspoon of the sugar with $1/4$ cup water (105° to 115°). Set aside for 10 minutes to soften. Combine eggs, shortening, remaining sugar, salt and $2^1/2$ cups flour with 1 cup water. Beat by hand or with mixer until smooth. Add enough remaining flour to make a soft dough. Cover and let rise until doubled in size, about 1 to $1^1/2$ hours. Punch down dough. (At this point you can shape into rolls, let rise and then bake or you can refrigerate dough.) If refrigerated, remove about 3 hours before baking. Shape into desired size rolls. Place on baking sheet and let rise until doubled in size, about 2 hours. Bake at 400° for 12 to 15 minutes or until lightly browned. Makes about 18 to 20 rolls.

ICE CREAM WITH AMARETTO

An elegant dessert and so quick and easy.

> **For each serving use:**
> **1 scoop vanilla ice cream**
> **Amaretto liqueur**
> **Sweetened whipped cream**
> **Sliced almonds**

Place one scoop of ice cream in each champagne glass or individual dessert dish. Spoon a small amount (depending on taste) of Amaretto over ice cream. Top with a spoonful of sweetened whipped cream; sprinkle with almonds.

Cranberry Chicken

Creamy Lemon Rice
Broccoli with Cheese Sauce
Tossed Salad with Mushrooms
Braided Bread Loaves
Vanilla Sherbet Dessert

Grocery List:

6 chicken breast halves
8 slices bacon
6 cups assorted salad greens
1 1/2 pounds fresh broccoli
2 cups fresh cranberries
1 lemon
1 orange
1/2 cup fresh mushrooms
1 cup long-grain rice
2 cups chicken broth
1/2 cup Garbanzo beans
1 package dry yeast
1/2 cup shredded coconut
Bottled Vinaigrette dressing
1 pint vanilla ice cream
1 pint pineapple sherbet
1 1/2 tablespoons Grand Marnier
   liqueur
1/2 cup whipping cream
2 ounces sharp Cheddar cheese
2 tablespoons grated Parmesan
   cheese

On Hand:

Salt and pepper
White pepper
1 1/4 cups sugar
5 cups flour
7 tablespoons oil
7 tablespoons butter
3 cups milk

Short Cut:

Serve broccoli without cheese
   sauce
Buy whole wheat rolls
Make dessert ahead and freeze

Serves 6

CRANBERRY CHICKEN   TOP OF STOVE

A wonderful recipe for the holidays.

> **6 chicken breast halves, skinned and boned**
> **$^1/_3$ cup flour**
> **3 tablespoons oil**
> **2 cups fresh cranberries**
> **$^3/_4$ cup sugar**
> **1 teaspoon salt**

Wash chicken and pat dry. Gently pound into cutlets about $^1/_4$-inch thick; coat with flour. Heat oil in heavy skillet and quickly brown chicken on both sides until golden. Remove chicken and drain off fat. Return chicken to skillet. Add remaining ingredients along with $^1/_3$ cup water; stir to blend. Bring to a boil; reduce heat and simmer about 20 minutes or until chicken is tender and sauce has thickened. Serve some of the sauce spooned over chicken. Makes 6 servings.

TIP: Be careful not to overcook the chicken or it will be tough and dry.

CREAMY LEMON RICE   TOP OF STOVE

Nice with almost any meal.

> **$^1/_4$ cup butter**
> **1 cup long-grain rice**
> **2 teaspoons freshly grated lemon peel**
> **2 cups chicken broth**
> **$^1/_2$ cup whipping cream**

Melt butter in a medium saucepan. Add rice and lemon peel. Cook over medium heat about 5 minutes, stirring occasionally. Add chicken broth. Cover and simmer 20 to 25 minutes or until liquid is absorbed. Add cream and continue to cook on low heat until cream is absorbed. Makes 6 servings.

VARIATION: You can omit the cream and have a nice light lemon flavored rice.

BROCCOLI WITH CHEESE SAUCE   TOP OF STOVE

A simple but elegant vegetable.

> 1^1/$_2$ pounds fresh broccoli, trimmed
> 3 tablespoons butter or margarine
> ^{1}/$_4$ cup flour
> 1^1/$_2$ cups milk
> ^{1}/$_2$ cup (2-ounces) grated sharp Cheddar cheese
> Salt and white pepper to taste

Steam broccoli until crisp tender. Meanwhile, melt butter in medium saucepan. Quickly stir in flour with a whisk; cook one minute. Remove from heat. Gradually stir in the milk until blended and smooth. Cook until thickened. Gradually stir in cheese, stirring to melt. Add salt and pepper to taste. Place broccoli on serving dish; top with some of the sauce. Pass remaining sauce with the broccoli. Makes 6 servings.

TOSSED SALAD WITH MUSHROOMS

> 6 cups assorted salad greens
> 8 slices bacon, cooked and crumbled
> ^{1}/$_2$ cup Garbanzo beans, drained
> ^{1}/$_2$ cup sliced fresh mushrooms
> Vinaigrette dressing
> Grated Parmesan cheese

When ready to serve, combine first 4 ingredients in large salad bowl. Toss with just enough dressing to lightly coat leaves. Arrange on salad plates; sprinkle lightly with grated Parmesan. Makes 6 servings.

BRAIDED BREAD LOAVES

Bread doesn't have to be difficult to make.

> 1$^{1}/_{2}$ cups milk
> 1 package dry yeast
> $^{1}/_{2}$ cup sugar
> 1 teaspoon salt
> $^{1}/_{4}$ cup oil
> 4$^{1}/_{2}$ cups flour

Heat milk until very warm but not hot. Pour into a large mixing bowl; stir in yeast, sugar and salt. Let stand 5 minutes. Add oil and 2 cups of the flour; beat well. Add 2 more cups of flour, using the remaining $^{1}/_{2}$ cup if needed to make a stiff dough. Knead on floured surface until smooth and elastic. Place in a large greased bowl; cover. Let rise in warm place until doubled in size, about 60 minutes.

Punch down dough. Divide in half and cut each half into 6 pieces. Roll each piece into about a 10-inch rope. Make 4 braids, using 3 ropes for each braid. Place one braid on top of the other and seal ends; repeat for second loaf. Place on greased baking sheets or in greased loaf pans. Let rise until double, 45 to 60 minutes. Bake at 350° for 30 to 35 minutes. If desired, brush top with butter; remove from pan and cool on rack. Makes 2 loaves.

VANILLA SHERBET DESSERT

A wonderful dessert you can prepare in a few minutes. Make the dessert just before serving, but toast the coconut ahead of time.

> 1 pint vanilla ice cream, softened slightly
> 1 pint pineapple sherbet, softened slightly
> 2 teaspoons finely grated fresh orange peel
> 1$^{1}/_{2}$ tablespoons Grand Marnier liqueur
> $^{1}/_{2}$ cup toasted shredded coconut

In large mixer bowl combine the first 4 ingredients; beat just until smooth and blended. Spoon into parfait, wine or champagne glasses. Sprinkle with toasted coconut. Serve immediately. Makes 6 servings.

TIP: Leftovers can be frozen. When frozen, the dessert has more body, but is equally as delicious.

Company Swiss Chicken

Steamed New Potatoes
Broccoli with Pecan Dressing
Lettuce Salad with Bananas
Sally Lunn Muffins
Apple Pie

Grocery List:

6 chicken breast halves
12 slices bacon
6 cups assorted salad greens
Parsley for garnish
6 ounces fresh mushrooms
Desired number tiny new
   potatoes
7 cups broccoli flowerettes
1 large banana
2 limes
6 to 7 tart apples
3 cups herb bread stuffing mix
3/4 cup pecans
1/3 cup walnuts
1 (9-inch) pie crust
6 ounces Swiss cheese

On Hand:

Salt and pepper
3 cups flour
2 cups sugar
3 teaspoons baking powder
1 teaspoon cinnamon
2 tablespoons mild-flavored
   honey
1/3 cup oil
2 1/4 cups butter
3 cups milk
2 eggs

Short Cut:

Serve hot buttered broccoli
Buy apple pie or serve ice cream

Serves 6

COMPANY SWISS CHICKEN

Everyone loves this recipe.

**6 chicken breast halves, skin removed
Salt and pepper
4 tablespoons melted butter or margarine, divided
12 slices bacon
6 ounces fresh mushrooms, sliced
1¹/₂ cups (6-ounces) Swiss cheese, grated**

Place chicken, skin side up, in a 9x13-inch baking dish. Sprinkle with salt and pepper. Pour 3 tablespoons of the melted butter over top. Bake at 350° for 40 minutes. Meanwhile, cook bacon. Drain on paper towels; crumble. Sauté mushrooms in remaining 1 tablespoon butter; drain. Remove chicken from oven. Combine bacon, mushrooms and cheese. Distribute over chicken, keeping as much of the mixture as possible on the chicken pieces. Bake 15 minutes. Makes 6 servings.

STEAMED NEW POTATOES

This is the best way to cook unpeeled whole new potatoes.

**Tiny new potatoes (desired number)
Butter
Parsley**

Place potatoes in steamer basket over boiling water. Cover; cook 15 minutes or until tender. Toss with butter and sprinkle with parsley. Serve immediately.

TIP: If potatoes are medium size, you may want to cut them in half.

PARSLEY

BROCCOLI WITH PECAN DRESSING

TOP OF STOVE
OVEN

Guests will go back for seconds with this recipe.

> 7 cups broccoli flowerettes (with 1^{1}/$_{2}$-inch stems)
> ^{1}/$_{2}$ cup plus ^{1}/$_{3}$ cup butter or margarine
> ^{1}/$_{4}$ cup flour
> 2 cups milk
> ^{3}/$_{4}$ cup pecans
> 3 cups herb bread stuffing mix

Steam broccoli until it starts to turn a bright green (do not cook until tender). Place in a buttered 7x11-inch baking dish. Heat ^{1}/$_{2}$ cup butter in medium saucepan. Add flour; mix well. Cook about one minute. Add milk; stir to blend. Cook over low heat, stirring frequently, until thickened. Pour evenly over broccoli. Melt remaining ^{1}/$_{3}$ cup butter. Combine butter with ^{2}/$_{3}$ cup water, pecans and stuffing mix. Spoon over broccoli. Bake at 400° for 30 minutes or until heated through and top is golden. Makes 6 to 8 servings.

LETTUCE SALAD WITH BANANAS

> 6 cups assorted salad greens
> 1 large banana, sliced
> ^{1}/$_{3}$ cup toasted chopped walnuts
> 2 tablespoons mild-flavored honey
> ^{1}/$_{3}$ cup salad oil
> ^{1}/$_{3}$ cup fresh lime juice

When ready to serve, combine salad greens, sliced bananas and walnuts in large salad bowl. Combine honey, oil and lime juice; mix well. Toss salad with just enough dressing to lightly coat leaves. Makes 6 servings.

SALLY LUNN MUFFINS
OVEN

A delicious light muffin. Best when served hot from the oven.

> **¹/₂ cup butter or margarine**
> **1 cup sugar**
> **2 eggs**
> **2 cups flour**
> **3 teaspoons baking powder**
> **1 cup milk**

In large mixer bowl, cream butter and sugar. Add eggs and mix thoroughly. Combine flour and baking powder. Add flour mixture to butter mixture, alternately with the milk, starting and ending with flour. Pour into greased muffin tins, filling three-fourths full. Bake at 400° for 18 to 20 minutes or until golden. Makes 12 muffins.

VARIATION: Bake in greased 9x5-inch loaf pan at 400° for 50 to 60 minutes. Let stand 5 minutes. Turn out on rack and serve or let cool.

FRENCH APPLE PIE
OVEN

> **1 (9-inch) unbaked pie crust**
> **6 to 7 tart apples, peeled and sliced**
> **1 cup sugar, divided**
> **1 teaspoon cinnamon**
> **³/₄ cup flour**
> **¹/₃ cup butter (chilled)**

Arrange apple slices in pie shell. Combine ¹/₂ cup sugar and cinnamon; sprinkle over apples. Combine remaining sugar and flour in small bowl. With fork or pastry blender, cut in butter until crumbly. Sprinkle evenly over apples. Bake at 400° for 40 minutes or until apples are tender. Makes 6 servings.

TIP: Although not a tart apple, the Golden Delicious makes a very good pie.

Golden Chicken with Garlic

Wild Rice with Pecans
Asparagus with Parmesan Cheese Sauce
Orange-Onion Romaine Salad
Oatmeal Casserole Bread
Cream Bruleé with Strawberries

Grocery List:

4 boneless chicken breast halves
$^1/_2$ pint fresh strawberries (opt)
2 seedless oranges
1 lemon
1 small red onion
1 pound asparagus
5 cups assorted salad greens
1 cup long-grain rice
$^1/_3$ cup wild rice
$3^2/_3$ cups chicken broth
1 (16-ounce) package Pillsbury Hot
   Roll mix
1 cup quick cooking oats
$^1/_2$ cup pecans
1 ounce Cheddar cheese
3 tablespoons grated Parmesan
   cheese
2 cups whipping cream

On Hand:

Salt and pepper
3 tablespoons light brown sugar
$^3/_4$ cup sugar
1 tablespoon flour
1 tablespoon vanilla extract
1 large whole head garlic
$5^1/_2$ tablespoons olive oil
4 tablespoons butter
$^1/_2$ cup milk
6 eggs

Short Cut:

Serve fresh asparagus with butter
Buy dinner rolls
Make Cream Bruleé day ahead

Serves 4

GOLDEN CHICKEN WITH GARLIC

TOP OF STOVE
OVEN

A quick and easy recipe that makes a delightfully different company dish.

> 4 chicken breast halves, skinned and boned
> 1 large whole head garlic
> 3 tablespoons olive oil
> 2 tablespoons fresh lemon juice
> 1 cup chicken broth

Wash chicken and pat dry. Separate cloves of garlic and remove papery skin (do not peel). Heat oil in heavy oven-proof skillet. Brown chicken and garlic about 4 minutes. Add lemon juice and chicken broth; bring to a boil. Place skillet in 400° oven and bake 20 minutes or until chicken is tender. Remove chicken and garlic; arrange on serving plate and keep warm. Cook liquid in skillet, over medium high heat, until reduced and mixture coats a spoon (stirring occasionally). Spoon sauce over chicken. Makes 4 servings.

TIP: Garlic becomes very mild and soft when cooked this way. It is delicious and not at all overpowering.

WILD RICE WITH PECANS

TOP OF STOVE

A perfect rice dish for a special company dinner.

> $^1/_3$ cup wild rice
> $2^2/_3$ cups chicken broth
> 1 cup long-grain rice
> $^1/_2$ cup coarsely chopped pecans
> 1 tablespoon butter or margarine

Wash wild rice well under cold running water for about a minute (this is easier to do in a strainer). In a medium saucepan, combine the wild rice and chicken broth. Bring to a boil. Reduce heat, cover and simmer 20 minutes. Add white rice and bring to a boil. Reduce heat, cover and simmer 20 minutes or until liquid is absorbed and rice is tender. Meanwhile, lightly toast pecans in heated butter. Gently stir pecans into the rice mixture. Makes 6 servings.

ASPARAGUS WITH PARMESAN CHEESE SAUCE   TOP OF STOVE

This recipe makes four servings, but if you have four people who love asparagus, you will need to double the recipe.

> 1 pound fresh asparagus
> 1 tablespoon butter or margarine
> 1 tablespoon flour
> $1/2$ cup milk
> $1/4$ cup (1-ounce) Cheddar cheese, grated
> 3 tablespoons freshly grated Parmesan cheese

Steam the asparagus until just crisp tender; the asparagus will turn a bright green and will usually take 5 to 6 minutes. Meanwhile, melt the butter in a small saucepan. Stir in flour; mix well and cook about a minute. Add milk and cook until thickened, stirring frequently. Gradually stir in the Cheddar cheese until melted and blended. Stir in Parmesan. Cook over low heat until smooth. Place asparagus in serving dish. Pour sauce over top. Makes 4 servings.

TIP: Fresh broccoli can be substituted for the asparagus.

VARIATION: The cheese sauce also makes a very good fondue served with French bread cubes. Just increase the recipe by desired amount.

ORANGE-ONION ROMAINE SALAD

One of my favorite quick salads with a light orange-flavored dressing.

> 4 to 5 cups assorted salad greens
> 4 thin slices red onion, separated into rings
> $1^1/2$ seedless oranges
> $2^1/2$ tablespoons olive oil
> $1^1/2$ teaspoons lemon juice
> Salt and pepper to taste

Place greens in salad bowl; add onion. Peel oranges and cut into thin slices. Take a couple of the slices and squeeze to get about $1^1/2$ teaspoons of juice. Cut remaining slices into quarters and add to salad. Combine orange juice with remaining ingredients; mix well. Add dressing to salad, adding just enough to lightly coat leaves; toss gently. Serve immediately. Makes 4 servings.

OATMEAL CASSEROLE BREAD

TOP OF STOVE
OVEN

An easy and quick batter-type bread with a delightful crunchy crust.

1 (16-ounce) package Pillsbury Hot Roll Mix
1 cup quick-cooking oats
3 tablespoons packed light brown sugar
2 tablespoons butter or margarine
2 eggs, lightly beaten

In large mixing bowl, from the mix, combine the yeast with the flour mixture, oats and brown sugar; mix well. In small saucepan, heat 1 cup water with the butter to 115° to 120°. Add to flour mixture along with the eggs; stir until well mixed and all the flour is moistened. Cover and let rise until doubled in size, about 45 minutes. Stir down dough; spoon into a greased 1¹/₂-quart casserole dish. Cover and let rise until doubled in size, about 30 minutes. Bake at 350° for 25 to 35 minutes or until well-browned and bottom crust sounds hollow when tapped. Remove and serve right away or cool on rack.

CREME BRULEÉ WITH STRAWBERRIES

TOP OF STOVE
OVEN, CHILL, BROIL

2 cups whipping cream
¹/₂ cup sugar plus some for top
4 egg yolks
1 tablespoon vanilla extract
Fresh strawberries (optional if not in season)

Pour cream into medium saucepan and heat over low heat until bubbles begin to form around edge of pan. Do not boil. In mixer bowl, beat sugar and egg yolks together until thick and light yellow, 2 to 3 minutes. Beating constantly, slowly add cream to egg mixture, adding a tablespoon at a time at first, then when egg mixture is thin, pour remaining cream in a steady stream. Add vanilla. Pour into custard cups or a quiche pan. Place in baking pan. Pour about an inch of boiling water into baking pan. Bake at 350° for 45 to 50 minutes or until custard is set and knife inserted just off center comes out clean. Remove from pan and chill at least 2 hours. Sprinkle top with a very thin layer of granulated sugar. Place under broiler and cook until sugar is melted and golden brown. Watch carefully, you don't want it to burn. Chill. Garnish with fresh strawberries. Makes 4 to 5 servings.

Orange-Almond Chicken

Barley Casserole
Green Beans Deluxe
Company Romaine Salad
Poppy Seed French Bread
Apple Crisp

Grocery List:

6 large chicken breast halves
1 large bunch romaine lettuce
5 medium Rome apples
3 oranges
1 onion
2 (16-ounce) cans green beans
1 cup pearl barley
3 cups chicken broth
6 tablespoons sliced almonds
$^1/_3$ cup slivered almonds
$^1/_3$ cup pecans, walnuts, or
    raisins
1 teaspoon poppy seeds
1 pint vanilla ice cream (opt.)
1 large loaf unsliced French
    bread
1 cup sour cream
2 ounces Swiss cheese

On Hand:

Salt and pepper
1 teaspoon cinnamon
$^1/_2$ teaspoon paprika
$^1/_4$ teaspoon garlic powder
$1^3/_4$ cups flour
1 cup sugar
1 large garlic clove
2 tablespoons cider vinegar
$1^1/_4$ cups butter
6 tablespoons olive oil

Short Cut:

Serve buttered fresh green beans
Prepare bread ahead, (but do not
    bake) wrap in foil

Serves 6

ORANGE ALMOND CHICKEN   OVEN
Especially good for a company meal.

6 large chicken breast halves, skinned
Salt and pepper
³/₄ cup flour
3 oranges (you will need ³/₄ cup juice, 1¹/₂ teaspoons peel)
6 tablespoons butter
6 tablespoons sliced almonds

Sprinkle chicken with salt and pepper. Coat with flour. Place in 9x13-inch baking dish. Squeeze ³/₄ cup juice from oranges. Grate 1¹/₂ teaspoons orange peel. Combine juice and peel; pour over chicken. Dot chicken with butter. Sprinkle with almonds. Bake at 350° for 60 minutes, basting 2 or 3 times during cooking time. Makes 6 servings.

BARLEY CASSEROLE   TOP OF STOVE
                                                          OVEN
A wonderful recipe that can be served with chicken, ham, pork, or beef. A nice change when you don't want rice or potatoes.

1 cup pearl barley
3 tablespoons butter or margarine, divided
¹/₃ cup slivered almonds
³/₄ cup finely chopped onion
Salt and pepper
3 cups chicken broth

Rinse barley and let drain. Meanwhile, heat 1 tablespoon butter in 10-inch skillet. Add almonds and lightly brown. Remove and set aside. Add remaining 2 tablespoons butter to skillet. Add onion and barley; cook until barley is lightly browned. Add almonds and just a dash of salt and pepper. Spoon into a greased 1³/₄-quart casserole. Bring chicken stock to a boil; pour over barley. Bake, uncovered, at 375° for 70 to 75 minutes or until liquid is absorbed and barley is tender. Makes 6 servings.

GREEN BEANS DELUXE

TOP OF STOVE
OVEN

2 (16-ounce) cans green beans, drained
$^1/_4$ cup finely chopped onion
$^1/_4$ cup butter or margarine
2 tablespoons flour
1 cup sour cream
$^1/_2$ cup (2-ounces) grated Swiss cheese

Place beans in a large mixing bowl. Melt butter in medium saucepan. Add onion; sauté just until soft. Stir in flour; cook 2 to 3 minutes. Remove from heat. Stir in sour cream and grated cheese. Pour over beans; toss to coat. Pour into greased 1$^1/_2$-quart casserole. Bake at 350° for 25 to 30 minutes or until heated through. Makes 6 servings.

COMPANY ROMAINE SALAD

CHILL

6 cups romaine lettuce
6 tablespoons olive oil
2 tablespoons apple cider vinegar
1 large garlic clove, peeled, thinly sliced
$^1/_2$ teaspoon salt
$^1/_8$ teaspoon freshly ground pepper

Wash romaine; tear into bite-size pieces and chill until ready to serve. Combine remaining ingredients; let stand at room temperature 1 to 2 hours. When ready to serve, remove garlic from dressing. Place romaine in salad bowl and toss with just enough dressing to coat. Makes 6 servings.

TIP: For an extra special dinner, garnish with cooked shrimp and sprinkle lightly with freshly grated Romano cheese.

POPPY SEED FRENCH BREAD

Don't plan on leftovers with this recipe.

> **1 large loaf unsliced French bread**
> **1 cup butter, melted**
> **1 teaspoon poppy seeds**
> **$^1/_4$ teaspoon garlic powder**
> **$^1/_2$ teaspoon paprika**

Trim crust from top and sides of bread. Slice lengthwise down the center, being careful to cut down to the bottom crust, but not through it. Cut across bread in $^1/_2$-inch slices, again being careful not to cut through the bottom crust. Combine remaining ingredients. Brush mixture over top and sides of bread and between the slices (depending on the size of the bread, you may not need all the butter mixture). Wrap bread in foil and set aside until just before serving. When ready to bake, fold foil down on all sides; place on baking sheet. Bake at 400° for 12 to 15 minutes or until golden brown. Serve on plate or basket and have guests pull off pieces of bread to eat. They will want to eat the bottom crust too, it is that good.

TIP: Can reheat in the oven, but not the microwave.

APPLE CRISP

Apple pie without the crust.

> **5 medium Rome apples, peeled (5 cups sliced)**
> **1 teaspoon cinnamon**
> **1 cup sugar**
> **$^3/_4$ cup flour**
> **$^1/_3$ cup butter (chilled)**
> **$^1/_3$ cup chopped pecans, walnuts or raisins (optional)**

Place sliced apples in buttered 9x9-inch baking dish. Sprinkle apples with cinnamon. Sprinkle 4 tablespoons water over apples. Combine sugar, flour and cut up pieces of butter in small mixing bowl. With fork or pastry blender, cut in the butter until crumbly. Add nuts. Sprinkle mixture evenly over apples. Bake at 350° for 40 to 45 minutes or until light golden and apples are tender. Makes 6 servings.

TIP: Delicious served warm with vanilla ice cream.

Marmalade Glazed Chicken

Swiss Potato Casserole
Butter Steamed Zucchini
Romaine and Artichoke Salad
Garlic Bread with Parmesan
Ice Cream Balls with Strawberries

Grocery List:

6 boneless chicken breast halves
1 quart strawberries
1 orange
2 medium tomatoes
6 medium potatoes
3 medium zucchini
1 bunch romaine lettuce
3/4 cup orange marmalade
1 (6 1/2-ounce) jar marinated artichoke hearts
1 cup sliced almonds
1 loaf unsliced French bread
1/2 gallon vanilla ice cream
1 1/2 cups whipping cream
5 ounces Swiss cheese
1 cup grated Parmesan cheese

On Hand:

Salt and pepper
1/8 teaspoon garlic powder
1/4 cup sugar
3/4 cup flour
2 tablespoons garlic red wine
  vinegar
4 1/2 tablespoons oil
6 tablespoons olive oil
3/4 cup plus 1 tablespoon butter

Short Cut:

Serve Steamed New Potatoes,
  page 142
Make ice cream balls ahead-freeze
Slice and sweeten strawberries

Serves 6

MARMALADE GLAZED CHICKEN   TOP OF STOVE

This is a favorite recipe you will want to make often. Quick and easy and ready to serve in about 30 minutes.

>   6 boneless chicken breast halves, skinned
>   ³/₄ cup flour
>   Salt and pepper
>   4¹/₂ tablespoons oil
>   6 tablespoons orange juice
>   ³/₄ cup orange marmalade

Gently pound chicken into cutlets, about ¹/₄-inch thick. Combine flour, salt and pepper. Dip chicken pieces in flour mixture, coating both sides. Heat oil in heavy skillet. Add chicken and brown both sides; this should take 3 to 4 minutes. Pour off oil. Combine orange juice and marmalade and pour over chicken. Cook, over low heat, until sauce thickens and chicken is glazed, basting frequently. Cooking time will be about 10 minutes. Makes 6 servings.

SWISS POTATO CASSEROLE   OVEN

Rich, but worth the calories.

>   6 medium potatoes, about 6 cups sliced
>   Salt and pepper
>   3 tablespoons butter, cut into small pieces
>   1¹/₄ cups (5-ounces) grated Swiss cheese
>   1¹/₂ cups whipping cream
>   ¹/₄ cup grated Parmesan cheese

Place half the potato slices in a greased 7x11-inch shallow baking dish. Sprinkle with salt and pepper, half the butter and half the Swiss cheese. Repeat with remaining half. Pour cream over top. Cover with foil; bake at 325° for 1 hour 15 minutes. Remove foil and bake 15 minutes. Sprinkle with the Parmesan cheese. Bake 15 minutes or until golden and potatoes are tender. Makes 6 servings.

BUTTER STEAMED ZUCCHINI   TOP OF STOVE

4 cups zucchini, sliced thin
2 tablespoons butter
4 tablespoons water
Salt and pepper

Wash zucchini and cut into thin slices, slightly less than $1/4$-inch. Melt butter in large skillet. Add zucchini and water. Cover and cook, over medium-high heat, stirring occasionally, until zucchini is just crisp tender. Drain off any liquid; season with salt and pepper. Makes 6 servings.

ROMAINE AND ARTICHOKE SALAD

A popular salad with almost any meal.

6 cups romaine lettuce
1 ($6^{1}/_{2}$-ounce) jar marinated artichoke hearts, drained
6 tablespoons olive oil
2 tablespoons garlic red wine vinegar
4 tablespoons grated Parmesan cheese, divided
12 sliced tomato wedges

Tear romaine into bite-size pieces; place in large salad bowl. Cut artichoke hearts into small bite-size pieces; add to romaine. Combine oil, vinegar and 2 tablespoons of the Parmesan cheese; mix well. Toss salad with just enough dressing to lightly coat leaves. Serve on salad plates; sprinkle with remaining Parmesan cheese. Garnish with tomato wedges. Makes 6 servings.

GARLIC BREAD WITH PARMESAN   BROIL

A slightly different twist to an old favorite.

$^1/_2$ **cup butter, softened**
$^1/_8$ **teaspoon garlic powder (or more to taste)**
$^1/_3$ **cup freshly grated Parmesan cheese**
1 loaf French bread

In mixer bowl, beat the butter for about a minute. Add garlic powder and Parmesan. Beat until well blended. Cut bread in half lengthwise. Spread halves with butter mixture (not too thick). Place under broiler, 5 to 6 inches from heat and toast until golden. This doesn't take very long, so watch carefully. Cut into slices.

ICE CREAM BALLS WITH STRAWBERRIES   FREEZE

Sweetened frozen strawberries can be substituted for the fresh .

Vanilla ice cream
1 cup sliced almonds
1 quart strawberries, sliced and sweetened

Quickly make 6 ice cream balls and roll in almonds. Cover and freeze until ready to serve. Place each ice cream ball in champagne glass or dessert dish. Top with strawberries.

VARIATIONS:
Ice cream, coconut and hot fudge sauce
Ice cream, sliced almonds and hot fudge sauce
Ice cream, chopped pecans and chocolate sauce
Ice cream, coconut and sweetened raspberries
Ice cream, coconut and Cherries Jubilee

Candied Chicken

Hot Buttered Rice
Petits Peas
Green Salad with Toasted Pecans
Sour Cream Muffins
Chocolate Mousse

Grocery List:

6 chicken breast halves
6 cups assorted salad greens
2 (10-ounce) packages frozen
  tiny peas
1¹/₂ cups long-grain rice
1 cup Log Cabin maple flavored
  syrup
1 (5-ounce) can sliced water
  chestnuts
¹/₂ cup pecans
6 (1-ounce) squares semi-sweet
  chocolate
¹/₂ cup sour cream
1 cup whipping cream

On Hand:

Salt and pepper
3 teaspoons baking powder
1 teaspoon vanilla extract
2 cups flour
¹/₂ cup plus 1 tablespoon sugar
¹/₄ cup powdered sugar
¹/₄ cup light brown sugar
¹/₂ cup white vinegar
¹/₄ cup red wine vinegar
¹/₂ cup catsup
³/₄ cup plus 2 tablespoons butter
¹/₂ cup olive oil
6 eggs

Short Cut:

Purchase muffins or dinner rolls
Make mousse day ahead

Serves 6

CANDIED CHICKEN

OVEN

A family favorite.

> **6 chicken breast halves**
> **Salt and pepper**
> **1 cup maple flavored syrup (Log Cabin)**
> **$^1/_2$ cup white vinegar**
> **$^1/_2$ cup catsup**
> **$^1/_4$ cup packed light brown sugar**

Sprinkle chicken with salt and pepper. Place, skin-side down, in greased or foil lined 9x13-inch baking pan. Combine remaining ingredients until blended. Pour over chicken. Cover with foil and bake at 325° for 1$^1/_2$ hours. Turn chicken. Bake, uncovered, 30 minutes, basting frequently to glaze chicken. Makes 6 servings.

TIP: Serve the chicken on a bed of rice; garnish with sprigs of parsley. Pass the sauce to serve over rice and chicken. Delicious.

HOT BUTTERED RICE

TOP OF STOVE

> **1$^1/_2$ cups long-grain rice**
> **1 teaspoon salt**
> **1$^1/_2$ tablespoons butter**

Bring 3$^1/_3$ cups water to a boil in medium-large saucepan. Stir in rice, salt and butter. Cover and simmer 15 to 20 minutes or until liquid is absorbed and rice is tender. Makes 6 servings.

MINT

PETITS PEAS   OVEN

Cook in oven along with the main dish.

> **2 (10-ounce) packages frozen tiny peas**
> **1 (5-ounce) can sliced water chestnuts, drained**
> **1 tablespoon sugar**
> **1 teaspoon salt**
> **¹/₈ teaspoon ground black pepper**
> **3 tablespoons butter or margarine**

Place frozen peas and water chestnuts in 1¹/₂-quart casserole. Sprinkle sugar, salt and pepper over top. Cut butter into tiny chunks; distribute over peas. Cover and bake at 350° for 60 minutes or until peas are thawed and heated through. Stir before serving. Makes 6 to 8 servings.

GREEN SALAD WITH TOASTED PECANS   TOP OF STOVE

An elegant salad you can make in just a few minutes.

> **6 cups assorted salad greens**
> **¹/₂ cup coarsely chopped pecans, toasted in a little butter**
> **¹/₂ cup olive oil**
> **¹/₄ cup red wine vinegar**
> **Salt and freshly ground pepper, to taste**

Place greens in large salad bowl. Add toasted pecans. Combine remaining ingredients; mix well. Add just enough of the dressing to lightly coat leaves. Makes 6 servings.

VARIATION: Add ¹/₂ cup mandarin orange slices or top each salad with about a tablespoon of tiny cooked shrimp.

SOUR CREAM MUFFINS   OVEN

Muffins are almost always best when served right out of the oven. These are slightly sweet with a nice crunch.

> 2 cups flour
> $^1/_2$ cup sugar
> 3 teaspoons baking powder
> $^1/_2$ cup butter (chilled)
> 2 eggs, slightly beaten
> $^1/_2$ cup sour cream

Combine the flour, sugar and baking powder in mixing bowl. Cut butter into tiny cubes; cut into flour mixture (with two dinner knives or a pastry blender) until it resembles small peas. Add eggs and sour cream; stir until all the flour is moistened (the batter will be quite stiff). Spoon into greased muffin tins filling about $^2/_3$ full. Bake at 425° for 18 to 20 minutes or until lightly browned and muffins test done. Makes 12 muffins.

CHOCOLATE MOUSSE   TOP OF STOVE
CHILL
Everybody loves a good chocolate mousse. This is a creamy, not too sweet, dense type mousse with a wonderful chocolate flavor.

> 6 (1-ounce) squares semi-sweet chocolate
> 4 eggs, separated
> 4 tablespoons powdered sugar, divided
> 1 cup whipping cream, divided
> 1 teaspoon vanilla extract, divided

Melt chocolate in heavy saucepan over very low heat. Remove from heat; stir until smooth. Pour into mixing bowl. Add egg yolks, one at a time, beating until smooth. Beat egg whites until foamy. Gradually add two tablespoons of the sugar and beat until whites hold their shape but are not stiff. Whip $^1/_2$ cup of the cream with $^1/_2$ teaspoon of the vanilla. Stir one-fourth of the egg whites into chocolate mixture. Fold in remaining egg whites and whipped cream, folding only until smooth. Spoon into custard cups or dessert glasses. Chill at least 3 hours or overnight. When ready to serve, whip remaining cream, sugar and vanilla; serve on mousse. Makes 6 servings.

Chicken Schnitzel

Fettuccine Romana
Honey Carrots
Italian Salad
Sourdough Bread
Coconut Pecan Cake

Grocery List:

4 boneless chicken breast halves
1 pound carrots
1 bunch green onions
5 cups assorted salad greens
1 small red onion
1 cup cherry tomatoes
$^1/_2$ cup frozen green peas
$^1/_2$ cup seasoned dry bread
   crumbs
6 ounces fettuccine noodles
2 (8-ounce) bottles Wishbone
   Italian dressing
1 (16-ounce) box light brown
   sugar
2 cups biscuit mix
1 (7-ounce) package Angel
   Flake coconut
1 cup pecans
1 pint vanilla ice cream
$^1/_3$ cup whipping cream
$^1/_2$ cup grated Parmesan cheese
1 loaf sourdough bread

On Hand:

Salt and pepper
2 tablespoons mild-flavored
   honey
$^3/_4$ cup butter
$^1/_2$ cup oil
1 tablespoon milk
6 eggs

Short Cut:

Serve pineapple sherbet with
crisp store-bought cookies

Serves 4

CHICKEN SCHNITZEL   TOP OF STOVE

An easier chicken recipe is hard to find. These are so tender you can almost cut them with a fork.

> **4 chicken breast halves, skinned and boned**
> **1 tablespoon milk**
> **1 egg**
> **$1/2$ cup seasoned dry bread crumbs**
> **4 tablespoons butter or margarine**

Place each chicken breast between wax paper; pound lightly to about $1/4$-inch thickness (you don't want them too thin). Beat milk and egg until well mixed. Dip chicken in egg mixture, then in bread crumbs to coat. Brown in heated butter in large skillet. Cook 3 to 4 minutes per side or until golden brown and tender. Makes 4 servings.

FETTUCCINE ROMANA   TOP OF STOVE

This makes a wonderful side dish with almost any main course, but it must be served right away. Cream, butter and Parmesan cheese should be at room temperature.

> **$1/3$ cup whipping cream**
> **$1/4$ cup butter**
> **$1/3$ cup freshly grated Parmesan cheese**
> **6 ounces fettuccine noodles**
> **$1/2$ cup frozen green peas**
> **Ground pepper to taste**

Let the first 3 ingredients stand at room temperature about an hour. Cook fettuccine according to directions on package. Add frozen peas during last 2 minutes of cooking time. Drain fettuccine and return to saucepan. Quickly stir in the cream, butter and cheese. Add pepper to taste. Serve at once. Makes 4 side servings or two main courses.

TIP: This may seem like too much work, but heated dinner plates will keep the fettuccine hot a lot longer. This can be done in your oven, but watch carefully and make sure your dishes are oven-proof. Also, some dishwashers have a cycle for heating plates.

VARIATION: For a delicious main course meal, add sautéed shrimp or chicken when adding other ingredients to the noodles.

HONEY CARROTS

TOP OF STOVE

A very nice carrot recipe with lots of color and so quick and easy to prepare you will want to make it often.

4 cups carrots, cut diagonally into 1-inch pieces
1 cup green onions, cut into 1-inch pieces
4 tablespoons butter or margarine
2 tablespoons mild-flavored honey
Salt and pepper to taste (optional)

In medium saucepan, cover carrots with water and cook until crisp tender, about 7 to 8 minutes. Add green onion and cook 1 minute. Drain well. Stir in butter and honey. Add salt and pepper, if desired. Makes 4 servings.

ITALIAN SALAD

The salad dressing is a local restaurant favorite.

5 cups assorted salad greens
1 small red onion, thinly sliced, separated into rings
1 cup cherry tomatoes, halved
2 (8-ounce) bottles Wishbone Italian dressing
1 egg, lightly beaten
3 tablespoons grated Parmesan cheese

Combine first 3 ingredients in large salad bowl. In small mixing bowl, combine remaining ingredients; mix well. Toss salad with just enough dressing to lightly coat leaves. Makes 4 servings.

TIP: Dressing can be made ahead and chilled. Makes enough dressing for several salads.

COCONUT PECAN CAKE

OVEN

Very rich!

> **4 eggs**
> **1 (16-ounce) box light brown sugar**
> **$^1/_2$ cup oil**
> **2 cups biscuit mix**
> **1 (7-ounce) package Angel Flake coconut**
> **1 cup chopped pecans**

In large mixer bowl, lightly beat eggs. Add brown sugar; mix well. Stir in oil. Add biscuit mix, a small amount at a time; mix well. Stir in coconut and pecans. Pour into an ungreased 9x13-inch baking pan. Bake at 325° for 40 to 45 minutes or until cake tests done. Let cool slightly; cut into 3-inch squares and serve with vanilla ice cream.

Cook's Tip

If a particular brand is specified in some of the recipes, it is because I have achieved the best results from that brand.

Company Chicken and Rice

Broccoli with Lemon Pepper
Romaine and Artichoke Salad
Herb Popovers
Coconut Lemon Pie

Grocery List:

12 chicken breast halves
2 bunches romaine lettuce
2 pounds broccoli
1 lemon
1 medium tomato
1¹/₂ cups Angel Flake coconut
1¹/₂ cups long-grain rice
1 can cream of celery soup
1 can cream of mushroom soup
1 can cream of chicken soup
1 (6¹/₂-ounce) jar marinated
   artichoke hearts
1 (4-ounce) package Garlic with
   Herbs cheese
5 tablespoons grated Parmesan
   cheese
1 (9-inch) pie crust

On Hand:

Salt and pepper
¹/₂ teaspoon lemon pepper
1 cup flour
1¹/₃ cups sugar
3 tablespoons garlic red wine
   vinegar
1¹/₂ cups butter
9 tablespoons olive oil
1 cup milk
5 eggs

Short Cut:

Purchase sourdough rolls
Serve ice cream with fresh berries

Serves 8

COMPANY CHICKEN AND RICE

OVEN

A favorite buffet dish.

> **12 chicken breast halves**
> **1¹/₂ cups uncooked long-grain rice**
> **1 can cream of celery soup**
> **1 can cream of mushroom soup**
> **1 can cream of chicken soup**
> **¹/₂ cup melted butter**

Place rice in bottom of large buttered roasting pan (pan should be at least 2-inches deep). Combine soups in mixing bowl; gradually stir in 1¹/₂ soup cans water, stirring to blend. Pour over rice. Dip chicken in butter; place, skin-side up, on rice mixture. Bake, uncovered, at 250° for 2¹/₂ hours or at 350° for 1¹/₂ hours or until liquid is absorbed, rice is tender and chicken has browned. Makes 8 to 12 servings.

TIP: You can add 1 (4-ounce) can sliced mushrooms and/or ¹/₂ cup slivered almonds.

BROCCOLI WITH LEMON PEPPER

TOP OF STOVE

A touch of lemon gives this a special flavor.

> **2 pounds fresh broccoli, trimmed**
> **4 tablespoons butter or margarine, melted**
> **¹/₂ teaspoon lemon pepper**
> **Lemon peel strips for garnish**

Steam broccoli until crisp tender, about 5 to 7 minutes. Place in serving dish. Combine melted butter and lemon pepper. Pour over broccoli and gently toss to coat. Sprinkle lemon peel over top. Makes 8 servings.

ROMAINE AND ARTICHOKE SALAD

A popular salad with almost any meal.

> 10 cups romaine lettuce, torn into bite-size pieces
> 1 (6¹/₂-ounce) jar marinated artichoke hearts, drained
> 9 tablespoons olive oil
> 3 tablespoons garlic red wine vinegar
> 5 tablespoons grated Parmesan cheese, divided
> 8 tomato wedges

Place romaine in large salad bowl. Cut artichoke hearts into small bite-size pieces; add to romaine. Combine oil, vinegar and 3 tablespoons of the Parmesan cheese; mix well. Toss salad with just enough dressing to lightly coat leaves. Serve on salad plates; sprinkle with remaining Parmesan cheese. Garnish with tomato wedge. Makes 8 servings.

HERB POPOVERS   OVEN

A delightful crunchy outside with an out-of-this-world flavor!

> 2 eggs
> 1 cup flour
> ¹/₂ teaspoon salt
> 1 cup milk
> 4¹/₂ teaspoons butter
> 1 (4-ounce) package Garlic with Herbs cheese, softened

Preheat oven to 425°. In mixer bowl, combine eggs, flour, salt and milk. Beat until well blended (may be slightly lumpy). Put ¹/₂ teaspoon butter in each of nine 2¹/₂-inch muffin tins. Place in oven to melt butter. Remove from oven and brush inside of tins with the butter to coat. Fill about one-third full with batter. Top with 1 teaspoon of the cheese. Pour remaining batter over the top, filling about two-thirds full. Bake 25 to 30 minutes or until puffed and browned. Serve immediately. Makes 9 popovers.

TIP: Leftover cheese can be served with crackers as a snack or, these popovers are so good, you may want to make them again within the next day or two.

COCONUT LEMON PIE

Similar to a pecan pie, but with coconut.

    1 (9-inch) pie crust
    $^1/_2$ cup butter or margarine, melted
    3 eggs, beaten
    $1^1/_3$ cups sugar
    4 teaspoons lemon juice
    $1^1/_2$ cups Angel Flake coconut

Combine melted butter, eggs and sugar; mix well. Add lemon juice and coconut. Pour into unbaked pie crust. Bake at 350° for 40 to 45 minutes or until knife inserted just off center comes out clean. Cool on rack. Makes 8 servings.

TIP: This is a very rich pie and should be cut into small servings.

Oven Baked Herb Chicken

Orange-Almond Rice
Fresh Vegetable Medley
Sweet-Sour Spinach Salad
Sourdough Rolls
Peach Melba

Grocery List:

1 chicken
8 slices bacon
1 large bunch spinach
1 lemon
1 orange
1 small red onion
1 cup green beans
1 cup carrots
1 small yellow squash
1 small zucchini
1 cup long-grain rice
$^{1}/_{2}$ cup slivered almonds
2 cups apple juice
1 (0.7-ounce) Good Seasons
   Cheese Garlic salad dressing mix
1 (16-ounce) can peach halves
1 pint vanilla ice cream
1 (10-ounce) package frozen
   raspberries
6 to 8 sourdough rolls
1 tablespoon grated Parmesan
   cheese

On Hand:

Salt and pepper
3 tablespoons sugar
2 tablespoons flour
3 tablespoons white vinegar
$^{3}/_{4}$ cup mayonnaise
$^{1}/_{2}$ cup plus 1 tablespoon butter

Short Cut:

Serve hot buttered rice or mashed
   potatoes
Purchase frozen peas in butter
   sauce

Serves 4

OVEN BAKED HERB CHICKEN   OVEN

This delicious herb-flavored chicken is so easy to prepare you will want to make it often. I guarantee your guests will want the recipe.

      1 chicken, cut up
      1 (0.7-ounce) package Good Seasons Cheese Garlic salad
         dressing mix
      2 tablespoons flour
      $1/4$ teaspoon salt
      $1/4$ cup butter or margarine, melted
      1 tablespoon fresh lemon juice

Place chicken, skin-side up, in shallow baking dish. Combine remaining ingredients; brush evenly over top of chicken. Bake at 350° for 60 minutes or until tender and browned. Makes 4 servings.

TIP: Best served hot from the oven. Do not freeze.

ORANGE-ALMOND RICE   TOP OF STOVE

A mild orange flavor.

      2 cups apple juice
      3 tablespoons butter, divided
      1 teaspoon salt
      1 cup long-grain rice
      $1/2$ cup slivered almonds
      1 tablespoon coarsely grated fresh orange peel

In medium saucepan, bring apple juice, 1 tablespoon of the butter and salt to a boil. Add rice. Bring to a boil, reduce heat, cover and simmer 20 to 25 minutes or until liquid is absorbed and rice is tender. Meanwhile, lightly brown almonds in the remaining butter. Remove almonds and set aside. When rice is cooked, gently stir in the almonds and orange peel. Makes 6 servings.

FRESH VEGETABLE MEDLEY   TOP OF STOVE

> 1 cup fresh green beans, trimmed
> 1 cup sliced carrots
> 1 cup sliced zucchini
> 1 cup sliced yellow squash
> 1^1/$_2$ tablespoons butter or margarine, melted
> Grated Parmesan cheese

Steam vegetables until just crisp tender (the zucchini and squash will cook much faster than the green beans and carrots). Toss with melted butter. Place vegetables in serving dish. Sprinkle with Parmesan cheese. Makes 4 servings.

TIP: If you want more color, omit the squash and add sliced red pepper.

SWEET-SOUR SPINACH SALAD   CHILL
                                               TOP OF STOVE

Guaranteed to be a winner every time.

> 1 large bunch fresh spinach
> 8 slices bacon, cooked and crumbled
> ^{3}/$_4$ cup mayonnaise
> 3 tablespoons sugar
> 3 tablespoons white vinegar
> 1 small red onion, thinly sliced, separated into rings

Wash spinach thoroughly. Remove stems; let dry. Tear into bite-size pieces and chill. Cook bacon. (This can be done ahead and chilled.) Combine mayonnaise, sugar and vinegar; chill. When ready to serve, combine spinach, bacon and onion in large salad bowl. Toss with just enough of the dressing to lightly coat leaves. Serve immediately. Makes 4 servings.

TIP: The dressing will make enough for about 3 recipes or you can decrease the ingredients. If the bacon is chilled, bring to room temperature before using or heat slightly.

PEACH MELBA

A nice light dessert.

1 (16-ounce) can peach halves, drained
1 pint vanilla ice cream
1 (10-ounce) package frozen raspberries, thawed

Place one peach half in each of 4 small serving dishes. Fill each center with a scoop of ice cream; top with some of the raspberries. Makes 4 servings.

TIP: To substitute, use fresh sweetened raspberries for the frozen, or use raspberry preserves.

Teriyaki Chicken

Fried Rice
Spinach Stir-fry with Almonds
Orange-Honey Salad
Hot Buttered French Bread
Grandma's Pound Cake

Grocery List:

1¹/₂ chickens
5 slices bacon
1 bunch romaine lettuce
3 bunches spinach
1 small piece fresh ginger
1 onion
2 green onions
2 limes
1 cup long-grain rice
¹/₃ cup pecans
¹/₃ cup slivered almonds
1 teaspoon sesame seeds (opt.)
1 (11-ounce) can mandarin
   oranges
1¹/₂ cups plus 2 tablespoons soy
   sauce
1 loaf French bread

On Hand:

Salt and pepper
1¹/₂ teaspoons vanilla extract
1¹/₂ teaspoons lemon extract
1 to 2 garlic cloves
2¹/₂ cups sugar
2 cups flour
2 tablespoons mild-flavored
   honey
³/₄ cup oil
1 cup butter
6 eggs

Short Cut:

Serve hot buttered rice
Purchase pound cake or Angel
   Food cake

Serves 6

TERIYAKI CHICKEN

TOP OF STOVE

You never know where you'll pick up a new recipe. This one is from my dentist's wife.

1¹/₂ chickens, cut up
1 cup soy sauce
1 tablespoon oil
¹/₂ cup sugar
1 to 2 garlic cloves, minced
5 thin slices fresh ginger

Wash chicken and pat dry, remove skin if desired. In a large wok or skillet, combine remaining ingredients. Cook over low heat until sugar is dissolved. Add chicken, skin-side down. Cover; simmer 30 minutes. Uncover; turn chicken and cook 30 minutes, basting frequently. Serve some of the sauce with the chicken. Makes 6 servings.

TIP: Leftover sauce can be used for chicken and beef kabobs. Marinate if you have time, if not, just baste several times when grilling.

FRIED RICE

TOP OF STOVE
CHILL

1 cup uncooked long-grain rice, cooked and chilled
5 slices bacon, cut into ¹/₂-inch pieces
³/₄ cup coarsely chopped onion
¹/₂ cup soy sauce
1 egg, beaten slightly
3 tablespoons chopped green onion, green part only

Partially cook bacon in large wok or skillet. Add onion; cook until tender but not brown. Stir in rice and soy sauce; cook until heated through, stirring occasionally. Push rice to the side. Pour egg into middle of pan. Stir to scramble, cooking until done. Stir egg into rice. Stir in green onion. Makes 6 servings.

VARIATION: Omit bacon, add diced cooked chicken, ham, pork or sausage. If desired, add 1 cup bean sprouts.

SPINACH STIR-FRY WITH ALMONDS   TOP OF STOVE

Don't overcook and you will enjoy this recipe even if you don't like cooked spinach.

> 3 bunches fresh spinach
> 4$\frac{1}{2}$ tablespoons oil
> $\frac{1}{3}$ cup slivered almonds
> 2 tablespoons soy sauce
> Sesame seeds (optional)

Remove stems from spinach; wash and dry. Heat oil in wok or Dutch oven. Add spinach and cook, stirring frequently, until leaves just start to wilt—this doesn't take long, so don't walk away from it. Add almonds and soy sauce. Spoon into serving bowl and sprinkle lightly with sesame seeds, if desired. Makes 6 servings.

ORANGE-HONEY SALAD

> 6 cups Romaine, torn into bite-size pieces
> 1 (11-ounce) can mandarin oranges, drained
> $\frac{1}{3}$ cup coarsely chopped pecans
> 2 tablespoons mild-flavored honey
> $\frac{1}{3}$ cup salad oil
> $\frac{1}{3}$ cup lime juice

When ready to serve, combine first 3 ingredients in large salad bowl. Combine honey, oil and lime juice; mix well. Toss salad with enough dressing to lightly coat leaves. Makes 6 servings.

GRANDMA'S POUND CAKE   OVEN

A family favorite that is best served same day made.

> **2 cups sugar**
> **2 cups flour**
> **1 cup butter or margarine, softened**
> **5 eggs**
> **1¹/₂ teaspoons vanilla extract**
> **1¹/₂ teaspoons lemon extract**

Combine all the ingredients in a large mixer bowl. Beat until very smooth, about 5 or 6 minutes. Pour into well-greased Bundt or Angel Food cake pan. Bake at 325° for 60 to 65 minutes or until cake tests done.

TIP: This is a delicious cake served warm or cold with ice cream, sweetened berries or sliced peaches.

Crunchy Chicken Strips

Baked Potatoes Raclette
Crisp Dinner Salad
Garlic Cheese Bread
Brownies with Ice Cream

Grocery List:

6 boneless chicken breast halves
5 cups assorted salad greens
1 medium tomato
4 medium baking potatoes
4 (1-ounce) squares un-
  sweetened chocolate
1 jar salsa
1 pint vanilla ice cream
16 ounces Monterey Jack cheese
1/4 cup grated Parmesan cheese
2 tablespoons Cheddar cheese
1 cup buttermilk
1 loaf French bread

On Hand:

Salt and pepper
1 teaspoon baking powder
1 garlic clove
2 cups sugar
3 1/4 cups flour
2 tablespoons red wine vinegar
2/3 cup shortening
6 tablespoons olive oil
Oil (1 to 1 1/2 cups)
1/2 cup butter
4 eggs

Short Cut:

Serve baked potatoes with
  butter and sour cream
Purchase sourdough rolls

Serves 4

CRUNCHY CHICKEN STRIPS   TOP OF STOVE

6 chicken breast halves, boned and skinned
Salt and pepper
2 cups flour
1 cup buttermilk
Oil

Cut chicken into 1-inch wide strips. Sprinkle with salt and pepper. Coat each strip with flour, dip in buttermilk, then coat again with flour. Heat about 1/2-inch of oil in large skillet. Fry chicken strips until golden on both sides and cooked through (do not overcook or they will be tough). Makes 4 servings.

BAKED POTATOES RACLETTE   OVEN
                                              BROIL

A different and delicious way to serve baked potatoes.

4 medium baking potatoes
1 pound Monterey Jack cheese
Salsa

Scrub potatoes; rub skin with oil for a crisp skin or wrap in foil for a soft skin. Bake at 400° for about an hour or until potatoes give easily when pressed. Meanwhile, cut cheese into 1/4-inch slices. Put in 9-inch pie plate. Place in oven during last 10 minutes of baking time. Remove potatoes from oven. Place cheese under broiler and broil 4 to 5 minutes, or until bubbly and lightly browned (watch carefully). Serve cheese over split baked potatoes; top with salsa. Makes 4 servings.

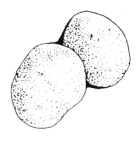

CRISP DINNER SALAD

Dressing can be made about 2 hours ahead.

5 cups assorted salad greens
6 tablespoons olive oil
2 tablespoons red wine vinegar
2 tablespoons grated Parmesan cheese, plus some for garnish
Salt and pepper to taste
1 medium tomato

Place salad greens in large salad bowl. Combine oil, vinegar, Parmesan cheese, salt and pepper. Toss salad with just enough dressing to lightly coat leaves. Place on chilled salad plates. Cut tomato into 8 wedges. Garnish each salad with 2 tomato wedges. Sprinkle lightly with Parmesan cheese. Makes 4 servings.

GARLIC CHEESE BREAD   OVEN

Delicious is the only way to describe this bread.

1 large garlic clove
$^1/_2$ cup butter, softened slightly
2 tablespoons grated Cheddar cheese
2 tablespoons grated Parmesan cheese
1 loaf French bread, sliced lengthwise

Place garlic clove in food processor or blender and process until minced. Add butter, Cheddar and Parmesan cheese. Process until blended and smooth. Spread on cut surface of bread (not too thick). Place on cookie sheet and bake at 450° for 4 to 5 minutes or until heated through and just beginning to crisp (top will not be brown). Cut into diagonal slices and serve.

BROWNIES   TOP OF STOVE
                                                    OVEN
Very rich and moist.

> 4 (1-ounce) squares unsweetened chocolate
> $^2/_3$ cup shortening
> 2 cups sugar
> 4 eggs, lightly beaten
> 1 teaspoon baking powder
> 1$^1/_4$ cups flour

Melt chocolate and shortening in saucepan over very low heat. Remove from heat; stir in sugar and eggs until blended. Add baking powder and flour; mix well. Pour into greased 9x13-inch baking pan. Bake at 350° for 25 to 30 minutes or until brownies start to pull away from sides of pan (do not overbake). Cool. Cut into squares or into 3-inch circles with a cookie cutter. Top with vanilla ice cream.

VARIATION: Cut brownies into small cubes and layer with the ice cream in parfait or dessert glasses.

Cook's Tip

It is easy to get in a rut and serve brownies the same way each time. Surprise your family by baking the above recipe in 2 (9-inch) pie pans. Spread with a thin layer of chocolate frosting and cut into pie-shaped wedges. For a brownie pizza, bake in a 12-inch pizza pan. Cool; drizzle with melted chocolate.

Easy Chicken Fettuccine

Italian Salad
Toasted Parmesan Sticks
Chocolate Mayonnaise Cake

Grocery List:

3 boneless chicken breast halves
6 cups assorted salad greens
1 small red onion
1 cup cherry tomatoes
2 (8-ounce) bottles Wishbone
    Italian dressing
1 (6-ounce) package semi-sweet
    chocolate chips
8 ounces Fettuccine noodles
2¹/₂ cups powdered sugar
1 cup whipping cream
1¹/₂ cups grated Parmesan cheese
1 loaf French or Italian bread

On Hand:

Salt and pepper
¹/₄ teaspoon white pepper
2 teaspoons baking soda
2 teaspoons vanilla extract
2 cups flour
1 cup sugar
4 tablespoons cocoa
1 cup mayonnaise
2 cups butter
¹/₄ cup milk
1 egg

Short Cut:

Make cake day ahead
Use canned chocolate frosting

Serves 4

EASY CHICKEN FETTUCCINE   TOP OF STOVE

Fettuccine isn't always an easy recipe to make, but you will like this one. No sauce to cook, just toss the ingredients with the hot noodles. The heat from the noodles will make the sauce. The first 3 ingredients must stand until room temperature, about 2 hours.

> $^{1}/_{2}$ **cup, plus 3 tablespoons butter**
> **1 cup whipping cream**
> **4 ounces (almost 1 cup) freshly grated Parmesan cheese**
> $^{1}/_{4}$ **teaspoon white pepper**
> **3 chicken breast halves, skinned and boned**
> **8 ounces Fettuccine noodles**

Place the $^{1}/_{2}$ cup butter, whipping cream and Parmesan cheese in large heavy skillet or saucepan. Cover and let stand until room temperature (about 2 hours). Just before serving, cut chicken breasts into strips or bite-size pieces and cook in remaining 3 tablespoons butter until golden and cooked through. Drain and set aside. Cook noodles as directed on package; drain, but do not wash. Immediately add to butter-cheese mixture; toss until evenly coated and sauce is blended. Stir in chicken. Makes 4 servings.

TIP: By omiting the chicken, this makes a nice side dish. If desired, add steamed zucchini slices.

ITALIAN SALAD

The salad dressing is a local restaurant favorite.

6 cups assorted salad greens
1 small red onion, thinly sliced, separated into rings
1 cup cherry tomatoes, halved
2 (8-ounce) bottles Wishbone Italian dressing
1 egg, lightly beaten
3 tablespoons grated Parmesan cheese

Combine first 3 ingredients in large salad bowl. In small mixing bowl, combine remaining ingredients; mix well. Toss salad with just enough dressing to lightly coat leaves. Makes 4 to 6 servings.

TIP: Dressing can be made ahead and chilled. Makes enough dressing for several salads.

TOASTED PARMESAN STICKS   OVEN

These bread sticks are delicious as a bread accompaniment to dinner or served with spaghetti, lasagna, soup or salad. Use a firm type bread such as French or Italian.

1 loaf unsliced French or Italian bread
1 cup butter or margarine, melted
¼ cup grated Parmesan cheese

Cut bread into 1-inch slices. Remove crusts. Cut each slice into strips about 1 inch wide. Combine melted butter and cheese. Brush mixture over all sides of the bread. Place on ungreased baking sheet. Bake at 325° for 15 to 20 minutes or until lightly toasted.

TIP: The amount of butter-cheese mixture needed may vary according to the size of the loaf of bread.

CHOCOLATE MAYONNAISE CAKE　　OVEN

This moist chocolate cake is perfect for a picnic or potluck dinner.

> **2 cups flour**
> **1 cup sugar**
> **4 tablespoons cocoa**
> **2 teaspoons baking soda**
> **1 cup mayonnaise**
> **1 teaspoon vanilla**

In mixer bowl, combine flour, sugar, cocoa and baking soda. Add mayonnaise, vanilla and $1^1/_2$ cups water. Beat, at medium speed, about one minute or until well mixed and smooth. Pour into greased 9x13-inch baking pan. Bake at 350° for 25 to 30 minutes or until cake tests done.

TIP: Frost with the following recipe or one of your family's favorite frostings.

CHOCOLATE FROSTING　　TOP OF STOVE

> **$^1/_4$ cup milk**
> **$^1/_4$ cup butter or margarine**
> **1 (6-ounce) package semi-sweet chocolate chips**
> **1 teaspoon vanilla extract**
> **$2^1/_2$ cups sifted powdered sugar**

Combine milk and butter in small saucepan. Bring to a boil; remove from heat. Stir in chocolate chips until melted and smooth. Place chocolate mixture in large mixing bowl. Add vanilla and powdered sugar. Beat to a spreading consistency. If necessary, add more powdered sugar to thicken or a few drops of milk to thin.

Chicken Enchiladas in Cream

Diablo Drink
Taco Chips and Salsa
Fresh Fruit Salad
Poppy Seed French Bread
Strawberry Mousse

Grocery List:

6 chicken breast halves
2 kiwi fruit
3 medium peaches
1 cantaloupe
1^1/$_2$ cups raspberries
^{1}/$_2$ cup blueberries
1 large banana
2 (10-ounce) packages frozen
  strawberries
1 (12-ounce) can frozen limeade concentrate
1 (8-ounce) can crushed pineapple
1 jar salsa
1 cup green chili salsa
1 (4-ounce) can chopped green
  chiles
1 (2 liter) bottle 7-UP
1^1/$_2$ cups white rum
1 teaspoon poppy seeds
1 (3-ounce) package strawberry
  jello

10 (8-inch) flour tortillas
1 large loaf unsliced French bread
1 bag taco chips
4^1/$_2$ cups whipping cream
8 ounces Monterey Jack cheese

On Hand:

Salt and pepper
^{1}/$_4$ teaspoon garlic powder
^{1}/$_2$ teaspoon paprika
1 teaspoon vanilla extract
^{1}/$_4$ cup sugar
1 cup butter

Short Cut:

Cook chicken breasts day ahead
Prepare bread ahead, (but do not
  bake) wrap in foil
Serve ice cream and cookies

Serves 6

CHICKEN ENCHILADAS IN CREAM   OVEN

A delicious casserole as well as attractive to serve.

> 3 cups cooked cubed chicken
> 1 cup green chili salsa (this is a red salsa)
> 1 (4-ounce) can chopped green chiles
> 10 (8-inch) flour tortillas
> 2$^1/_2$ cups whipping cream
> 2 cups (8-ounces) grated Monterey Jack cheese

Combine chicken, salsa and green chiles. Fill each tortilla with a portion of the chicken mixture. Roll up and place, seam-side down, in greased 9x13-inch baking dish. Pour cream over top. Sprinkle evenly with cheese. Bake at 350° for 45 minutes or until golden and most of the cream is absorbed. Makes 6 servings.

DIABLO DRINK

A refreshing party drink on a hot summer day or evening.

> 1 (12-ounce) can frozen limeade concentrate
> 1 juice can white rum
> Chilled 7-UP, approximately 2 liters, or to taste
> Crushed pineapple, drained
> Ice cubes

In large pitcher, combine limeade concentrate (do not dilute) and rum. Add 7-Up to taste. To each glass or punch cup, add a little crushed pineapple and ice cubes. Pour rum mixture over top.

FRESH FRUIT SALAD

Substitute other fruits if not in season.

1¹/₂ **cups sliced peaches**
1¹/₂ **cups raspberries**
1¹/₂ **cups cubed cantaloupe**
1 **cup sliced bananas**
¹/₂ **cup sliced kiwi**
¹/₂ **cup blueberries**

Combine fruit and gently toss to mix. Makes 6 servings.

POPPY SEED FRENCH BREAD   OVEN

Don't plan on leftovers with this recipe.

1 **large loaf unsliced French bread**
1 **cup butter, melted**
1 **teaspoon poppy seeds**
¹/₄ **teaspoon garlic powder**
¹/₂ **teaspoon paprika**

Remove crust from top and sides of bread. Slice lengthwise down the
center, being careful to cut down to the bottom crust, but not through
it. Cut across bread in ¹/₂-inch slices, again being careful not to cut
through the bottom crust. Combine remaining ingredients. Brush
mixture over top and sides of bread and between the slices (depending on the size of the bread, you may not need all the butter mixture).
Wrap bread in foil and set aside until just before serving. When ready
to bake, fold foil down on all sides; place on baking sheet. Bake at 400°
for 12 to 15 minutes or until golden brown. Serve on plate or basket
and have guest pull off pieces of bread to eat. They will want to eat the
bottom crust too, it is that good.

TIP: Can reheat in the oven, but not the microwave.

EASY STRAWBERRY MOUSSE   CHILL

Serve as a light dessert.

> 1 (3-ounce) package strawberry jello
> 1 cup boiling water, 1 cup cold water
> 2 cups whipping cream
> 1/4 cup sugar
> 1 teaspoon vanilla extract
> 2 (10-ounce) packages frozen strawberries, thawed, drained

Combine jello with one cup boiling water until dissolved. Add cold water. Place in refrigerator until cool but not set. Whip cream with the sugar and vanilla. Add drained strawberries to jello. Fold in whipped cream. Pour into champagne or parfait glasses or dessert dishes. Chill overnight to set. Makes 10 to 12 servings.

TIP: The strawberries tend to sink, so remember to scoop to the bottom to evenly distribute among each dessert. If fresh strawberries are in season, garnish with whipped cream and top with a strawberry. For 5 to 6 servings make half the recipe using only half of the box of jello.

Brunch

———————

Chicken Quiche Pizza
Fresh Fruit Bowl
Cinnamon Rolls
Coffee - Orange Juice

Grocery List:

2 chicken breast halves
8 slices bacon
6 cups assorted fruit for salad
2 loaves frozen white bread
  dough
Orange juice
Coffee
1 (9-inch) pie crust
8 ounces Swiss cheese
1^1/$_3$ cups sour cream
^{1}/$_2$ cup whipping cream

On Hand:

2 teaspoons cinnamon
^{3}/$_4$ cup sugar
1 cup light brown sugar
^{1}/$_2$ cup butter
4 eggs

Short Cut:

*Thaw bread dough in refrigerator
overnight*

Serves 6

CHICKEN QUICHE PIZZA

Delicious! You will need a 12-inch pizza pan for this recipe.

> **One 9-inch pie crust**
> **8 slices bacon, cooked and crumbled**
> **1 cup small cubed cooked chicken**
> **2 cups (8-ounces) grated Swiss cheese**
> **1$^1/_3$ cups sour cream**
> **4 eggs**

Roll pastry into a 13-inch circle. Place in 12-inch pizza pan. Fold edges over, pressing against sides, forming a thicker crust. Bake at 425° for 5 minutes. Let cool. Sprinkle bacon and chicken over crust. Top with grated cheese. Combine remaining ingredients; mix well. Pour evenly over cheese. On lowest rack of oven, bake 20 to 25 minutes or until set and just starting to brown. Makes 6 servings.

TIP: While pizza is baking, make salad with the assorted fruits. To save time, use store-bought prepared pie crust.

KATHY'S CINNAMON ROLLS

Gooey, rich and delicious. These will disappear fast.

> **2 loaves frozen bread dough, thawed**
> **$^1/_2$ cup butter, melted**
> **1 cup firmly packed light brown sugar**
> **$^3/_4$ cup sugar**
> **2 teaspoons cinnamon**
> **$^1/_2$ cup whipping cream**

Cut each loaf into 8 equal pieces. Roll into 8-inch long strips. Combine butter and brown sugar; mix well. Spread evenly in 9x13-inch baking dish. Combine sugar and cinnamon; mix well. Quickly dip each strip of bread dough in water, then roll in cinnamon-sugar to coat. Tie in a loose knot; place in baking dish. Pour cream over top. Bake at 350° for 30 to 35 minutes or until golden. Carefully invert onto a large pan or platter. For more attractive rolls, invert again so that the golden side is up. Spoon some of the sauce over top. Makes 16 rolls.

TIP: To save time, cover and thaw bread dough overnight in refrigerator. Dough will be ready to use the next morning. No rising time is needed in this recipe.

Mom's Fried Chicken

Mashed Potatoes
Cream Gravy
Fresh Vegetable Medley
Colonial Inn Pea Salad
Buttermilk Biscuits
Peach Cobbler

Grocery List:

2 chickens
1¹/₂ cups green beans
1¹/₂ cups carrots
2 small zucchini
2 small yellow squash
8 medium potatoes
1 lemon
1 small onion
1 head lettuce
2 cups frozen peas
¹/₂ gallon vanilla ice cream
1 quart sliced peaches, fresh or
  canned
1 cup Bisquick
1 tablespoon grated Parmesan
  cheese
4 ounces Swiss or Cheddar
  cheese
1 cup plus 2 tablespoons buttermilk

On Hand:

Salt and pepper
¹/₈ teaspoon baking soda
2 tablespoons baking powder
3¹/₄ cups flour
1 cup sugar
¹/₂ cup plus 3 tablespoons
  butter
2 cups oil (approximately)
6 tablespoons mayonnaise
4 cups milk
2 eggs

Short Cut:

Serve hot buttered frozen peas
  or broccoli
Purchase canned refrigerated
  biscuits

Serves 6

MOM'S FRIED CHICKEN   TOP OF STOVE

We all have favorite foods from our childhood and I remember Mom's fried chicken as the best.

>   2 chickens, cut up
>   2 eggs, slightly beaten
>   1 cup milk
>   1 cup flour
>   Salt and pepper
>   Oil

Combine eggs and milk; mix well. Combine flour, salt and pepper. Dip chicken in milk mixture, then in flour mixture to coat. Heat 1 to 1¹/₂--inches oil in deep skillet. Oil should be hot, about 350°. Add chicken, skin-side down. Cover and cook 15 minutes. Turn chicken. Cover and cook 10 to 15 minutes or until chicken is nicely browned and cooked through. Makes 6 servings.

CREAM GRAVY   TOP OF STOVE

>   4 tablespoons fat from frying chicken
>   4 tablespoons flour
>   2 cups milk
>   Salt and pepper

Leave 4 tablespoons fat in pan along with the crusty bits that stick to the bottom. Heat until hot. Stir in flour until blended. Cook until lightly browned and bubbly, stirring constantly. Add milk; stir to mix well. Continue cooking, stirring frequently, until gravy is thickened, about 5 minutes. Add salt and pepper to taste. Makes 2 cups.

TIP: If gravy is too thick, stir in a little milk. If too thin, add a little flour mixed with a small amount of water.

NOTE: Start cooking the potatoes before you start the chicken. When ready to serve, mash with a little butter, milk, salt and pepper.

FRESH VEGETABLE MEDLEY   TOP OF STOVE

$1^1/_2$ cups fresh green beans, trimmed
$1^1/_2$ cups sliced carrots
$1^1/_2$ cups sliced zucchini
$1^1/_2$ cups sliced yellow squash
3 tablespoons butter or margarine, melted
Grated Parmesan cheese

Steam vegetables until just crisp tender (the zucchini and squash will cook much faster than the green beans and carrots). Toss with melted butter. Place vegetables in serving dish. Sprinkle with Parmesan cheese. Makes 6 servings.

COLONIAL INN PEA SALAD   CHILL

Salad must chill at least 8 hours or overnight.

6 tablespoons mayonnaise
3 tablespoons fresh lemon juice
$^1/_4$ cup finely chopped onion
1 cup (4-ounces) grated Swiss or Cheddar cheese
2 cups frozen peas (do not thaw)
5 cups lettuce, torn into bite-size pieces

Combine mayonnaise and lemon juice; mix well. Add onion, grated cheese and peas. Cover and refrigerate 8 hours or overnight. Just before serving, add lettuce and toss to mix. Makes 6 to 8 servings.

VARIATION: Add 4 slices bacon, cooked and crumbled and/or $^1/_2$ cup sliced water chestnuts.

BUTTERMILK BISCUITS   OVEN

2 cups flour
2 tablespoons baking powder
$^1/_2$ teaspoon salt
$^1/_8$ teaspoon baking soda
1 cup, plus 2 tablespoons buttermilk
$^1/_4$ cup oil

In large mixing bowl, combine flour, baking powder and salt. Add baking soda to buttermilk. Add to flour mixture and stir just until moistened. Turn out on lightly floured surface and knead 3 or 4 times or just until smooth. Pat dough into $^1/_2$-inch thick round. Cut with 2-inch cutter, cutting straight down, do not twist. Dip in oil and place in baking pan, edges touching. Bake at 500° for 8 to 10 minutes or until golden brown. Makes 12 to 14 biscuits.

TIP: If you don't want a crunchy bottom, place biscuits in pan and brush tops only with the oil.

VARIATION: For Whipping Cream Biscuits:
2 cups flour
1 tablespoon sugar
1 tablespoon baking powder
1 teaspoon salt
1$^1/_4$ cups whipping cream
$^1/_4$ cup melted butter or margarine (for dipping)
Follow above instructions for mixing; bake at 425° for 10 to 12 minutes.

PEACH COBBLER   OVEN

So fattening, but so good!

$^1/_2$ cup butter, melted
1 cup Bisquick mix
1 cup sugar
1 cup milk
1 quart sliced peaches, fresh or canned
Vanilla ice cream

Pour melted butter into a 7x11-inch baking dish. Stir in Bisquick, sugar and milk. Pour peaches over top. Bake at 375° for 35 to 40 minutes or until golden. Serve warm with vanilla ice cream. Makes 6 servings.

Park or Patio Picnic

_____

Skillet Fried Chicken
Macaroni Salad
Picnic Coleslaw
Pineapple Baked Beans
Brownie Cupcakes
Walnut Shortbread

Grocery List:

2 chickens
6 slices bacon
1 small onion
3 stalks celery
1 small head cabbage
1 Golden Delicious apple
1 cup red seedless grapes
$1/2$ cup sweet pickles plus $1/2$ cup
    juice
1 (8-ounce) package salad
    macaroni
$1/2$ cup pecans
$2^1/4$ cups walnuts
1 (8-ounce) can crushed
    pineapple
2 (16-ounce) cans pork and beans
4 (1-ounce) squares unsweetened
    chocolate

On Hand:

Salt and pepper
$1/2$ teaspoon thyme
1 teaspoon dry mustard
2 teaspoons vanilla extract
6 cups flour
3 cups plus 2 tablespoons sugar
$1/2$ cup light brown sugar
$1/2$ cup catsup
3 cups butter
Oil (about $1^1/2$ to 2 cups)
3 cups mayonnaise
4 eggs

Short Cut:

Fry chicken ahead
Purchase macaroni salad
Omit Walnut Shortbread

Serves 6

SKILLET FRIED CHICKEN   TOP OF STOVE

There must be hundreds of ways to fix fried chicken! This method is very quick and easy and requires very little attention while cooking.

> 2 chickens, cut up
> 1 cup flour
> 2 teaspoons salt
> $^1/_2$ teaspoon ground black pepper
> $^1/_2$ teaspoon thyme
> Oil

Combine flour, salt, pepper and thyme. Coat chicken with flour mixture. Pour $^1/_2$ inch of oil in electric skillet (do not heat). Add chicken pieces, skin-side down. Cover the pan and turn control to 350°. When you can hear the oil sizzling loudly, cook chicken 15 minutes (do not lower heat). Remove the cover and turn chicken. Cook, uncovered, 8 to 10 minutes or until chicken is done. Drain on paper towels. Makes 6 servings.

TIP: If you don't have an electric skillet, use a regular skillet and cook on top of the stove. The heat should be high enough to hear the oil sizzling.

MACARONI SALAD   TOP OF STOVE
                                                            CHILL

> 5 cups cooked salad macaroni
> $^1/_2$ cup finely chopped onion
> $^3/_4$ cup chopped celery
> $^1/_2$ cup chopped sweet pickles (save $^1/_2$ cup juice)
> 2 cups mayonnaise
> Salt and pepper to taste

In large mixing bowl, combine macaroni, onion, celery and pickles. In small bowl, combine the $^1/_2$ cup pickle juice and mayonnaise; mix well. Add about three-fourths of the mayonnaise to macaroni. Add salt and pepper to taste. Cover and chill several hours or overnight. Also chill the remaining dressing. The chilled macaroni will absorb most of the mayonnaise. Toss with a little additional dressing before serving. Makes 6 to 8 servings.

VARIATION: Add chopped cooked eggs, pimiento or sliced black olives.

PICNIC COLESLAW   CHILL

Lots of color and crunch.

> **6 cups shredded cabbage**
> **1 Golden Delicious apple, cubed**
> **1 cup red seedless grapes, halved**
> **$^1/_2$ cup coarsely chopped pecans or small pecan halves**
> **2 tablespoons sugar (or to taste)**
> **1 cup mayonnaise**

Combine first 4 ingredients in large mixing bowl. Combine sugar and mayonnaise, stirring to dissolve sugar. Add just enough dressing to cabbage mixture to lightly coat. Cover and chill until ready to serve. Makes about 10 to 12 servings.

PINEAPPLE BAKED BEANS   OVEN

> **1 (8-ounce) can crushed pineapple, drained**
> **2 (16-ounce) cans pork and beans**
> **$^1/_2$ cup firmly packed light brown sugar**
> **1 teaspoon dry mustard**
> **$^1/_2$ cup catsup**
> **6 slices bacon, diced**

Combine first 5 ingredients. Pour into greased 1$^1/_2$-quart casserole. Top with diced bacon. Bake at 325° for 2 to 2$^1/_2$ hours. Makes 6 servings.

BROWNIE CUPCAKES   OVEN

A favorite with adults as well as children.

> **4 (1-ounce) squares unsweetened chocolate**
> **1 cup butter or margarine**
> **2 cups sugar**
> **4 eggs**
> **1 cup flour**
> **1$^1/_4$ cups chopped walnuts**

In saucepan, melt chocolate and butter over very low heat. Stir to blend. Remove from heat. Add sugar; mix well. Stir in eggs and flour. Add walnuts. Pour into paper-lined muffin tins, filling three-fourths full. Bake at 350° for 25 to 30 minutes or until tests done (watch carefully at this point and don't overbake). Makes 16 cupcakes.

WALNUT SHORTBREAD   OVEN

Shortbread can be addictive —you keep going back for more. This is a large recipe, but will keep for several days if tightly covered.

> **2 cups (1 pound) butter, softened**
> **1 cup sugar**
> **1 cup walnuts, finely ground**
> **2 teaspoons vanilla (white vanilla, if you have it)**
> **$^1/_4$ teaspoon salt**
> **4 cups flour**

In large mixer bowl, cream butter and sugar until light and fluffy. Add walnuts, vanilla and salt; mix well. Add flour and mix until blended. Spoon into greased 10x15x1-inch baking pan. Spread evenly. Bake at 325° for 35 to 45 minutes or until light and golden. Cool and cut into small bars or squares.

TIP: Walnuts can be finely ground in a blender or food processor. Some of the more expensive vanillas can slightly darken a light batter so use a clear white vanilla, if you have it on hand.

Thanksgiving

———

Cup of Cheer Hot Drink	Yam and Apple Casserole
Apricot Almond Brie	Green Peas in Butter Sauce
Stuffed Turkey or	Cranberry Sauce
Roast Chicken	Green Salad with Toasted Pecans
Sausage Bread Stuffing	Jiffy Dinner Rolls
Mashed Potatoes	Pumpkin Pie
Turkey Gravy	Pecan Pie

Grocery List:

12 pound turkey
$^3/_4$ pound bulk sausage
12 cups assorted salad greens
1 large onion
$^3/_4$ cup celery
6 medium yams
8-10 medium potatoes
6 tart apples
12 ounces fresh cranberries
1 cup light corn syrup
6 cups grapefruit juice
4 cups orange juice
4 cups apple cider
$^1/_2$ cup apricot preserves
1 tablespoon sliced almonds
1$^3/_4$ cups pecans
9 ounce box white Jiffy cake mix
1 package dry yeast
1 cup chicken broth
3 packages frozen peas
1 (12-ounce) can evaporated milk
1 (16-ounce) can pumpkin
1 (8-ounce) package herb bread
   stuffing mix

1 tablespoon Grand Marnier
   liqueur
1 (10-inch) deep-dish pie crust
1 (9-inch) pie crust
2 (8-ounce) wedges Brie cheese

On Hand:

Salt and pepper
12 whole cloves
2 (2-inch) cinnamon sticks
1$^1/_2$ teaspoons pumpkin pie spice
3 tablespoons cornstarch
3$^1/_2$ cups flour
4$^1/_4$ cups sugar
5 eggs
2 cups butter
$^3/_4$ cup olive oil
6 tablespoons red wine vinegar
2 large sheets heavy duty foil

Short Cut:

Make cranberry sauce ahead
Buy dinner rolls
Make pies day before

Serves 8

CUP OF CHEER HOT DRINK   TOP OF STOVE

1 cup sugar
12 whole cloves
2 (2-inch) pieces cinnamon sticks
6 cups grapefruit juice
3 cups orange juice
4 cups apple cider

In small saucepan, combine sugar, cloves and cinnamon sticks with $^1/_2$ cup water. Bring to a boil; reduce heat and simmer 20 minutes. Remove cloves and cinnamon sticks. In large pan or kettle, combine juices and apple cider; stir in sugar syrup. Heat gently until hot (do not boil). Serve hot. Makes 26 punch cup servings.

TIP: Will keep up to 2 weeks in refrigerator. Remove amount needed; heat and serve.

APRICOT ALMOND BRIE   TOP OF STOVE

Elegant but very quick and easy. Serve with a plain type cracker.

2 (8-ounce) wedges Brie cheese
$^1/_2$ cup apricot preserves
1 tablespoon Grand Marnier liqueur
1 tablespoon toasted sliced almonds

Remove top rind from cheese. Place cheese on serving plate. In small saucepan, combine preserves and liqueur. Heat until mixture is hot, but do not boil. Pour some of the sauce over cheese. Sprinkle almonds over top. Makes 8 servings.

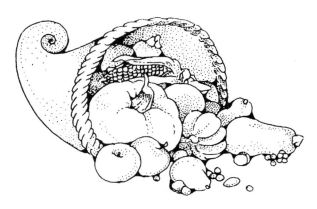

FOIL-WRAPPED TURKEY OVEN

Turkey
Wide heavy duty foil
Oil or melted butter

Cut 2 long strips of foil. Place one piece lengthwise in large shallow roasting pan and one piece crosswise in pan. Place turkey, breast side up, on top of foil. Brush with oil or butter. Bring 2 opposite ends of foil up over turkey; fold ends together to seal. Bring remaining two ends of foil up and seal. Bake at 450°:

8-10 pounds	$2^1/_4$-$2^1/_2$ hours
10-12 pounds	$2^3/_4$-3 hours
14-16 pounds	3-$3^1/_4$ hours
18-20 pounds	$3^1/_4$-$3^1/_2$ hours
22-24 pounds	$3^1/_2$-$3^3/_4$ hours

For stuffed turkeys, you may find it necessary to cook 30 minutes longer. To brown turkey, open foil during last 30 minutes of cooking time. To test for doneness, meat thermometer should read 185° or thickest part of drumstick should move up and down easily. Close foil and let stand 15 minutes before carving.

TIP: This is my favorite way to bake turkey. Basting is eliminated and it provides lots of turkey stock for gravy. Baking time is much quicker.

SAUSAGE BREAD STUFFING TOP OF STOVE

$^3/_4$ pound bulk sausage
$^1/_2$ cup butter or margarine
$1^1/_4$ cups coarsely chopped onion
$^3/_4$ cup chopped celery
1 (8-ounce) package herb seasoned bread stuffing mix
1 cup chicken broth

Brown sausage in large skillet. Drain off fat; place sausage in large mixing bowl. Melt butter in the skillet. Add onion and celery; cook until soft but not brown. Combine onion mixture with sausage and stuffing mix. Pour broth over top and gently mix until well coated. Use to stuff turkey or bake in a casserole. Makes enough for a 12 pound turkey.

VARIATION: About $^1/_2$ cup coarsely chopped pecans make a nice addition.

TURKEY GRAVY   TOP OF STOVE

$^1/_2$ cup fat drippings
$^1/_2$ cup flour
4 cups turkey stock (from turkey or from cooking giblets)
Salt and pepper

When turkey is done, pour meat juices into large measuring cup. Remove $^1/_2$ cup of fat that rises to the top. Pour into medium saucepan. (Discard remaining fat.) Heat fat until hot. Stir in flour; cook over low heat until lightly browned. Add turkey stock, stirring constantly to blend. Cook, stirring frequently, over medium heat, until thickened and smooth. Season to taste with salt and pepper. Makes 4 cups.

TIP: If too thin, stir in additional flour mixed with a small amount of water or stock. If you don't have 4 cups turkey stock, add water to make up the difference.

YAM AND APPLE CASSEROLE   TOP OF STOVE
                                              OVEN

Delicious served with turkey or ham.

6 yams, cooked and peeled (or use canned)
6 tart apples, peeled
$^1/_2$ cup butter or margarine
2 cups water
1 cup sugar
3 tablespoons cornstarch

Cut yams and apples in $^1/_2$-inch slices. Cut rounds in half crosswise. Layer in buttered 3-quart deep casserole, starting with apples and ending with yams. Combine butter and water in medium saucepan. Bring to a boil. Mix sugar with cornstarch; add just enough cold water to make a paste. Add to boiling water mixture, stirring constantly. Bring to a boil; remove from heat. Pour over yams. Bake at 350° for 50 to 60 minutes or until apples are tender. Makes 12 servings.

NOTE: Start the potatoes after the above recipe goes in the oven. When ready to serve, mash with a little milk, butter, salt and pepper.

CRANBERRY SAUCE   TOP OF STOVE

1 cup sugar
1 cup orange juice
12 ounces fresh or frozen cranberries

Combine sugar and orange juice in medium saucepan. Bring to a boil and cook until sugar is dissolved. Add cranberries and cook 8 to 10 minutes. The cranberries will burst, causing a popping sound. Remove from heat and cool slightly. Cover and chill. Makes $2^1/2$ cups.

GREEN SALAD WITH TOASTED PECANS   TOP OF STOVE

12 cups assorted salad greens
$^3/_4$ cup coarsely chopped pecans, toasted in a little butter
$^3/_4$ cup olive oil
6 tablespoons red wine vinegar
Salt and freshly ground pepper, to taste

Place greens in salad bowl. Add pecans. Combine remaining ingredients; mix well. Add enough dressing to coat leaves. Makes 8 servings.

JIFFY DINNER ROLLS
                                                      OVEN

1 (9-ounce) box white or yellow Jiffy cake mix
1 package dry yeast
$^1/_2$ teaspoon salt
$1^1/_4$ cups hot tap water
$2^1/_2$ to 3 cups flour

In large mixing bowl, combine cake mix, yeast and salt. Stir in water and flour to make a soft dough. (Dough will be quite sticky.) Cover and let rise until double, 1 to $1^1/2$ hours. Stir down dough and spoon onto a well-floured surface. Gently turn dough a couple times to lightly coat with flour. Shape into desired size rolls and place on greased baking sheets. Or shape into balls and place in greased muffin tins. Cover and let rise until double, about 1 hour. Bake at 400° for 10 to 15 minutes or until golden. Makes 15 to 18 rolls depending on size desired.

PUMPKIN PIE

OVEN

An all-time holiday favorite.

> **1 (10-inch) deep dish pie crust**
> **1 (16-ounce) can pumpkin**
> **1 (12-ounce) can evaporated milk**
> **³/₄ cup sugar**
> **1¹/₂ teaspoons pumpkin pie spice**
> **2 eggs, beaten**

There is a lot of filling, so make sure the edges are crimped high on the pie shell. Combine remaining ingredients; blend well. Pour into pie shell. Bake at 425° for 15 minutes. Reduce heat to 350°; continue baking 45 to 50 minutes or until a knife inserted near the center comes out clean. Let cool; refrigerate until ready to serve. Makes 6 to 8 servings.

TIP: If pie crust is browning too fast, cover edges with narrow strips of foil.

PECAN PIE

OVEN

> **1 (9-inch) pie crust**
> **¹/₄ cup butter or margarine**
> **¹/₂ cup sugar**
> **3 eggs, beaten**
> **1 cup light corn syrup**
> **1 cup coarsely chopped pecans**

Cream butter and sugar until light. Add eggs and corn syrup; mix well. Stir in pecans. Pour into pie crust. Bake at 350° (325° if using glass pie plate) for 40 to 45 minutes or until knife inserted just off center comes out clean. Place on rack and cool. Makes 6 servings.

TIP: If crust browns too quickly, cover edges with narrow strips of foil.

Christmas Menu

Holiday Eggnog Punch	Company Rice Casserole
Pineapple Cheese Ball	Romaine and Shrimp Salad
Onion Soup with Brie	Refrigerator Dinner Rolls
Gourmet Baked Chicken	Heavenly Cheesecake
Broccoli with Pecan Dressing	Almond Toffee Crunch
Butter-Glazed Acorn Squash	Raisin-Pecan Chocolate Bark

Grocery List:

5 whole chicken breasts, boned
6 ounces tiny shrimp
2 small bunches romaine
2 pounds broccoli (approx.)
1 small green pepper
4 large onions
3 to 4 acorn squash
2 packages dry yeast
3/4 cup raisins
1 (8-ounce) can crushed pineapple
1 (7-ounce) box Konriko brand
   Wild Pecan Rice
1/2 cup dark rum
1 quart vanilla ice cream
12-ounces milk chocolate chips
12-ounces semi-sweet chocolate chips
1 1/2 cups pecans
2 cups pecans or walnuts
1 cup slivered almonds
3 cups graham cracker crumbs
1 1/2 cups dry bread crumbs
7 1/2 cups chicken broth
3 cups herb bread stuffing mix
1 (2 liter) bottle 7-UP or Sprite
1/2 gallon commercial eggnog
6 (8-ounce) packages cream cheese
8 ounces Brie cheese

2 cups sour cream
1/4 cup grated Parmesan cheese

On Hand:

Salt and pepper
1 1/4 teaspoons paprika
1 tablespoon seasoning salt
3 teaspoons dried parsley
2 teaspoons vanilla extract
1 tablespoon Worcestershire sauce
4 1/4 cups sugar
4 3/4 cups flour
1/2 cup light brown sugar
2 tablespoons light corn syrup
1/4 cup red wine vinegar
2 tablespoons mild-flavored honey
3/4 cup olive oil
3 1/2 cups butter
1/2 cup shortening
2 cups milk
7 eggs

Short Cut:

Omit soup
Purchase dinner rolls
Serve hot buttered fresh broccoli

Serves 6 to 8

HOLIDAY EGGNOG PUNCH

This is a very popular non-alcoholic eggnog recipe for the holidays.

> $^1/_2$ **gallon commercial eggnog**
> **1 quart vanilla ice cream, softened**
> **1 (2 liter) bottle 7-UP or Sprite**

Combine eggnog and ice cream in a large punch bowl. Gently stir in the Sprite or 7-UP.

TIP: This is a large recipe that will serve at least 12 to 14 people (depending on how much they drink). If you have a small group, make half the recipe. The punch doesn't keep after the fizz goes out of the pop.

PINEAPPLE CHEESE BALLS   CHILL

A most requested recipe during the holidays. Can make 2 days ahead.

> **2 (8-ounce) packages cream cheese, softened**
> **1 (8-ounce) can crushed pineapple, drained**
> **2 cups finely chopped pecans or walnuts**
> $^1/_4$ **cup finely chopped green pepper**
> **2 tablespoons finely chopped onion**
> **1 tablespoon seasoning salt**

In mixer bowl, beat cream cheese until smooth. Add crushed pineapple, 1 cup of the nuts, green pepper, onion and salt; mix well. (If using food processor, do not overmix.) Cover and chill until firm enough to shape. Divide mixture in half; shape into balls and roll in remaining 1 cup of nuts. Cover and chill several hours or overnight. Serve with assorted crackers. Makes 2 cheese balls.

TIP: Leftover cheese balls can be reshaped and rolled in additional nuts. For a variation from the traditional cheese ball, place mixture in small serving bowl or crock and serve at room temperature. (Do not use the second cup of nuts.)

ONION SOUP WITH BRIE   TOP OF STOVE

A nice cold weather soup with a mild onion-cheese flavor.

> $^1/_4$ **cup butter or margarine**
> **6 cups thinly sliced onions, separated into rings.**
> **1 teaspoon sugar**
> **5 cups well-seasoned chicken broth**
> **8 ounces Brie cheese, rind removed**
> **Salt to taste**

Heat butter in Dutch oven or large saucepan. Add onion; sprinkle with sugar. Sauté 15 to 20 minutes or until onions are tender. Add chicken broth. Cut Brie into small cubes and add to mixture. Cook over low heat until cheese is melted, stirring frequently. Add salt to taste. Makes 6 to 8 servings.

TIP: For added color, sprinkle with a little parsley just before serving. If you don't have homemade chicken broth, use 3 (14$^1/_2$-ounce) cans regular strength chicken broth.

GOURMET BAKED CHICKEN   MARINATE
                                                          CHILL, OVEN
Must be started day ahead.

> **5 whole chicken breasts, halved, boned, skinned**
> **2 cups sour cream**
> **1 tablespoon Worcestershire sauce**
> **2 teaspoons salt**
> **1$^1/_4$ teaspoons paprika**
> **1$^1/_2$ cups fine dry bread crumbs**

Place chicken in shallow baking dish. Combine sour cream, Worcestershire sauce, salt and paprika; pour over top. Turn chicken to coat. Cover and refrigerate overnight. Next day, drop chicken pieces, one at a time in bread crumbs, turning to coat. Shape each piece to make a nice round fillet. Place in buttered baking pan. Cover and chill at least 1$^1/_2$ hours. Bake at 325° for about 1$^1/_4$ hours or until golden and tender. (While baking, if chicken looks dry, baste with a little melted butter.) Makes 6 to 8 servings.

TIP: There is extra chicken in case someone wants seconds. (Also good cold the next day.)

BROCCOLI WITH PECAN DRESSING

TOP OF STOVE
OVEN

Guests will go back for seconds with this recipe.

7 cups broccoli flowerettes (with 1^1/$_2$-inch stems)
^{1}/$_2$ cup plus ^{1}/$_3$ cup butter or margarine
^{1}/$_4$ cup flour
2 cups milk
^{3}/$_4$ cup pecans
3 cups herb bread stuffing mix

Steam broccoli until it starts to turn a bright green (do not cook until tender). Place in a buttered shallow 2-quart baking dish. Heat ^{1}/$_2$ cup butter in medium saucepan. Add flour; mix well. Cook about one minute. Add milk; stir to blend. Cook over low heat, stirring frequently, until thickened. Pour evenly over broccoli. Melt remaining ^{1}/$_3$ cup butter. Combine butter with ^{2}/$_3$ cup water, pecans and stuffing mix. Spoon over broccoli. Bake at 400° for 30 minutes or until heated through and top is golden. Makes 6 to 8 servings.

BUTTER-GLAZED ACORN SQUASH

OVEN

3 to 4 acorn squash, cut in half, seeds removed
8 tablespoons butter, melted
^{1}/$_2$ cup packed light brown sugar
^{1}/$_2$ cup dark rum
2 tablespoons mild-flavored honey

Place squash, cut side down, on a greased shallow baking pan. Bake at 350° for 30 minutes. Remove from oven and turn squash, cut side up. Spoon 1 tablespoon butter into each cavity. Combine brown sugar and rum; mix well. Add about a tablespoon of mixture to each cavity. Brush sides and tops of squash with the sauce. Bake 15 to 20 minutes or until tender. Remove from oven; pour off liquid. Brush with a light coating of honey. Makes 6 to 8 servings.

VARIATION: Just before serving, fill each cavity with hot buttered peas or Chinese peas and water chestnuts.

COMPANY RICE CASSEROLE

This is a delightful rice casserole with a slightly nutty taste. It can be served with almost any type of main dish.

> 3 tablespoons butter
> 1 cup finely chopped onion
> 1 (7-ounce) box Wild Pecan Rice (Konriko brand)
> 1 teaspoon salt
> 3 teaspoons dried parsley
> 2$^1/_2$ cups chicken broth

Heat butter in medium size skillet. Add onion; cook about one minute. Add rice; cook 3 to 4 minutes or until onion is soft, stirring occasionally. Pour into a greased 2$^1/_4$ or 2$^1/_2$-quart deep casserole. Stir in remaining ingredients. Cover and bake at 375° for 50 to 60 minutes or until liquid is absorbed and rice is tender. Gently stir to distribute the parsley that floats to the top. Makes 6 to 8 servings.

ROMAINE WITH SHRIMP SALAD

> 8 cups romaine lettuce, torn into bite-size pieces
> 6 ounces tiny shrimp, cooked
> $^3/_4$ cup olive oil
> $^1/_4$ cup red wine vinegar
> $^1/_4$ cup grated Parmesan cheese
> Salt and pepper

In large salad bowl, toss romaine with the shrimp. Combine remaining ingredients. Toss salad with just enough dressing to lightly coat leaves. Place on individual chilled salad plates. If desired, sprinkle with additional Parmesan cheese. Makes 6 to 8 servings.

REFRIGERATOR DINNER ROLLS   OVEN

You will find this recipe convenient when you have a busy week, but still want delicious homemade rolls for a special dinner. Dough can be made ahead and refrigerated overnight.

2 packages dry yeast
3 eggs, beaten lightly
$^1/_2$ cup shortening
$^1/_2$ cup sugar
1$^1/_2$ teaspoons salt
4$^1/_2$ cups flour

Combine yeast and 1 teaspoon of the sugar with $^1/_4$ cup water (105° to 115°). Set aside for 10 minutes to soften. Combine eggs, shortening, remaining sugar, salt and 2$^1/_2$ cups flour with 1 cup water. Beat by hand or with mixer until smooth. Add enough remaining flour to make a soft dough. Cover and let rise until doubled in size, about 1 to 1$^1/_2$ hours. Punch down dough. (At this point you can shape into rolls, let rise and then bake or you can cover and refrigerate dough.) If refrigerated, remove about 3 hours before baking. Shape into desired size rolls. Place on baking sheet and let rise until doubled in size, about 2 hours. Bake at 400° for 12 to 15 minutes or until lightly browned. Makes about 18 to 20 rolls.

I gave a little tea party
This afternoon at three
'Twas very small
three guests in all
I, myself and me
Myself ate up the sandwiches
While I drank all the tea
'Twas also I who ate the pie
And passed the cake to me

Author unknown

HEAVENLY CHEESECAKE

OVEN
CHILL

Everyone loves cheesecake and this is one of the best. Can make 2 days ahead.

3 cups graham cracker crumbs
$^3/_4$ cup butter or margarine, melted
4 (8-ounce) packages cream cheese, softened
1$^2/_3$ cups sugar
4 large eggs, beaten slightly
2 teaspoons vanilla extract (white vanilla if possible)

Combine graham cracker crumbs and melted butter; mix well. Press onto bottom and up sides of a 9-inch springform pan. In large mixer bowl, beat cream cheese until smooth. Add sugar and beat until very smooth. Add eggs and vanilla; beat until smooth. Carefully pour into springform pan. Bake at 300° for 1 hour 20 minutes or until center no longer moves when pan is gently shaken. Watch carefully the last few minutes, you want to remove as soon as the center is set. Remove from oven and let cool on rack. Cover and refrigerate at least 8 hours before serving. Makes 12 servings.

VARIATIONS: If you like to serve a topping on your cheesecake, serve Pineapple Jubilee, page 132, Cherries Jubilee, sweetened strawberries or raspberries, blueberry sauce or cherry pie filling. If you like a sour cream topping: Combine 1 cup sour cream, $^1/_4$ cup sugar and 2 tablespoons fresh lemon juice. When done, remove cheesecake from oven and carefully spoon sour cream mixture evenly over top. Return to oven and bake 5 minutes. Cool on rack and refrigerate at least 8 hours.

ALMOND TOFFEE CRUNCH

TOP OF STOVE
CHILL

1 cup butter
1¹/₄ cups sugar
2 tablespoons light corn syrup
1 cup toasted slivered almonds
1 (12-ounce) package milk chocolate chips

In heavy medium-size saucepan, combine the butter, sugar, corn syrup and 2 tablespoons water. Cook over medium heat, stirring frequently, until mixture comes to a boil. Cook to 300° on candy thermometer. Remove from heat; stir in almonds. Pour into foil-lined 10x15-inch jelly roll pan. Sprinkle chocolate chips over top. Let stand 5 minutes or until soft. Spread evenly over toffee, making swirls across the top. Cool. Chill about an hour. Break into small pieces.

TIP: To substitute, use milk chocolate candy bars for the chips.

RAISIN-PECAN CHOCOLATE BARK

TOP OF STOVE
CHILL

Can be prepared in less than 10 minutes.

1 (12-ounce) package milk chocolate chips
1 tablespoon shortening
³/₄ cup raisins
³/₄ cup chopped pecans, divided

In heavy small saucepan, carefully melt chocolate chips and shortening over low heat; stir to blend. Remove from heat; stir in raisins and ¹/₄ cup of the pecans. Pour into buttered, then wax paper-lined 7x11-inch baking dish; spread evenly. Sprinkle with remaining ¹/₂ cup pecans; press lightly. Chill about 45 minutes to set. Break into small pieces.

VARIATION: By substituting semi-sweet chocolate for the milk chocolate, you will get a darker, slightly less sweet candy.

Index

GREAT MEALS BEGIN WITH SIX INGREDIENTS OR LESS

Six Ingredients Or Less Cookbook - over 500 recipes from everyday cooking to delicious company entertaining. Sections include: Appetizers, Breads, Cookies, Desserts, Beef, Seafood, Poultry, Vegetables and many more.

Six Ingredients Or Less Chicken Cookbook - dedicated to a familiar and favorite standby, from appetizers, salads, and main dishes to 20 complete menus for plan-ahead dining.

If you cannot find **Six Ingredients Or Less** or **Six Ingredients Or Less Chicken Cookbook** at your local store, order directly from C.J. Books. Copy and fill out the order blank below and return, with your check or money order to:

SIX INGREDIENTS OR LESS
P.O. Box 922
GIG HARBOR, WA 98335

Remember, Cookbooks Make Great Gifts!

(Birthdays, Christmas, Mother's Day, Weddings, Showers, House warmings, Thank yous, Campers, Boaters)

Six Ingredients Or Less	(_____# of copies)	$10.95 each	$_____
Six Ingredients Or Less Chicken Cookbook	(_____# of copies)	$10.95 each	$_____
Plus postage & handling		$1.25 each	$_____
Subtotal			$_____
Washington residents add sales tax		.95 each	$_____
Total			$_____

PLEASE PRINT OR TYPE

NAME_____

ADDRESS_____

CITY_____STATE_____ZIP_____

Six Ingredients Or Less Cookbook - over 500 recipes from everyday cooking to delicious company entertaining. Sections include: Appetizers, Breads, Cookies, Desserts, Beef, Seafood, Poultry, Vegetables and many more.

Six Ingredients Or Less Chicken Cookbook - dedicated to a familiar and favorite standby, from appetizers, salads, and main dishes to 20 complete menus for plan-ahead dining.

If you cannot find **Six Ingredients Or Less** or **Six Ingredients Or Less Chicken Cookbook** at your local store, order directly from C.J. Books. Copy and fill out the order blank below and return, with your check or money order to:

SIX INGREDIENTS OR LESS
P.O. BOX 922
GIG HARBOR, WA 98335

Remember, Cookbooks Make Great Gifts!

(Birthdays, Christmas, Mother's Day, Weddings, Showers, House warmings, Thank yous, Campers, Boaters)

Six Ingredients Or Less	(_____ # of copies)	$10.95 each	$_____
Six Ingredients Or Less Chicken Cookbook	(_____ # of copies)	$10.95 each	$_____
Plus postage & handling		$1.25 each	$_____
Subtotal			$_____
Washington residents add sales tax		.95 each	$_____
Total			$_____

PLEASE PRINT OR TYPE

NAME_____

ADDRESS_____

CITY_____STATE_____ZIP_____